The American Frugal Housewife

Edited by
Lydia Maria Child

With a New Introduction by
Janice (Jan) Bluestein Longone

DOVER PUBLICATIONS
Garden City, New York

Bibliographical Note

This Dover edition, first published in 1999, is an unabridged
and unaltered republication of the twenty-ninth edition of *The
American Frugal Housewife, Dedicated to Those Who Are Not Ashamed
of Economy,* originally published by Samuel S. & William Wood,
New York, in 1844. A new Introduction has been written specially
for the Dover edition by Janice (Jan) Bluestein Longone.

Library of Congress Cataloging-in-Publication Data

Child, Lydia Maria Francis, 1802–1880.
    The American frugal housewife / edited by Lydia Maria
Child.
        p. cm.
    Reprint of the 29th ed. Originally published: New York :
Wood, 1844.
    ISBN-13: 978-0-486-40840-8 (pbk.)
    ISBN-10: 0-486-40840-X (pbk.)
    1. Home economics. 2. Cookery. I. Title.

TX147 .C53 1999
640—dc21

                                                          99-052199

Manufactured in the United States of America
40840X13   2022
www.doverpublications.com

Introduction to the Dover Edition

Lydia Maria Child, the author of *The Frugal Housewife, Dedicated to Those Who Are Not Ashamed of Economy*, was one of 19th-century America's most influential women. This book of cookery and household management was first published in Boston (March & Capen and Carter & Hendee) in 1829. By the eighth edition of 1832, its title was changed to *The American Frugal Housewife* so as not to confuse it with an earlier English work, *The Frugal Housewife*, by Susannah Carter, first published in London in 1765 and in Boston in 1772. Mrs. Child's eighth edition most pointedly informs the reader that the title was changed to differentiate her book from that English work which was "not adapted to the wants of this country."

"The wants of this country"—in this case, an American cookbook using American ingredients and conditions, especially for those in need, were always uppermost in Mrs. Child's thoughts.

The American Frugal Housewife quickly became the standard American cookbook of its time, following in the footsteps of Amelia Simmons' *American Cookery* (1796) and Mary Randolph's *The Virginia Housewife* (1824). It was reprinted at least thirty-five times between 1829 and 1850 when it was allowed to go out of print because of Mrs. Child's increasingly public work, unpopular in some quarters, in the cause of anti-slavery, and because of the publication of newer, more modern books. It is sobering to note, however, that her work was reprinted *in England* as late as 1860.

Lydia Maria Francis Child was born on February 11, 1802 in Medford, Massachusetts, the youngest of six children of Susannah Rand and Convers Francis, a baker and businessman. From her parents she learned to live simply and to be generous to others. Her lifelong credo was that "all true excellence and happiness consist in living for *others*, not for *yourselves*."

The dominant influence of her early years was her brother Convers who, being male, was given the Harvard education Lydia Maria always wished she had had. By fifteen years of age she was reading *Paradise Lost* and writing to her brother of Milton's misogyny and male chauvinism. Women's rights and the rights of the poor, especially of black and native Americans, were to be dominant themes of her long and productive life.

In 1824 she published her first novel *Hobomok*, which catapulted her to instant fame. The novel was daring in a number of ways: it was one of the earliest books to help define a distinctive American literature and it dealt with the unmentionable subject of a white woman's marriage to an American Indian. Two years later came *The Rebels*, a tale of the American Revolution.

In 1826 she founded the *Juvenile Miscellany*, the first American monthly periodical for children, and for the next several years, she wrote short stories and articles for a variety of newspapers and magazines.

She married the improvident David Lee Child, a Boston lawyer in 1829. From then on, due to the legal and social problems arising from their work in the abolitionist movement (including David's imprisonment and large debts), Lydia Maria became the family breadwinner.

Thus, a work for "those not ashamed of economy" seemed a natural next book to the author, both to help the American housewife during the hard times following the recession of the 1820's and to help the Childs pay their bills.

Mrs. Child could indeed be frugal—and a bit severe. Assuredly, this was the result of the Puritan ethic in which she was raised as well as her own personal experiences.

In her introduction, she sets the tone of the book:

> The true economy of housekeeping is simply the art of gathering up all fragments, so that nothing be lost. I mean fragments of *time*, as well as *materials*.

> Nothing should be thrown away so long as it is possible to make any use of it, however trifling that use may be.

> Whatever the size of a family, every member
> should be employed, either in earning or saving
> money.
>
> In this country, we are apt to let children romp
> away their existence, till they get to be thirteen or
> fourteen. This is not well.
>
> I have attempted to teach how money can be *saved*,
> not how it can be *enjoyed*.
>
> Look frequently to the pails, to see that nothing is
> thrown to the pigs which should have been in the
> grease-pot. Look to the grease-pot, and see that
> nothing is there which might have served to nour-
> ish your own family, or a poorer one.

That last line, about helping others poorer than yourself, is perhaps the key to Lydia Maria Child. This woman cared about that "poorer" family. She did, in fact, devote most of her life to those less able to help themselves or to raise themselves out of poverty and humiliation, whether these were due to slavery or to prejudicial laws and education policies.

In addition to hundreds of recipes from Apple Pie to Whortleberry Pudding, *The American Frugal Housewife* contains household hints, medical remedies, practical information on buying, cooking, and storing food, and moral and social observations on the role and education of women. This latter section included the opinion that marriage was not the end-all and be-all for females.

Although many of the recipes are for economical cooking, the touch of a knowledgeable cook is often obvious. Her dough-nut recipe is flavored with cinnamon, rose-water, or lemon-brandy. Her Raspberry Shrub is "a pure, delicious drink for summer . . . a good economy to make it answer instead of Port and Catalonia wine." Her Wedding Cake calls for three pounds of butter, four pounds of currants, two pounds of raisins, twenty-four eggs, half a pint of brandy, one ounce of mace, and three nutmegs, among other ingredients. Nothing "frugal" here.

Lydia Maria expected even a poor household to have and be able to use a surprising variety of herbs, spices, and seasonings. Her recipes call for allspice, caraway seeds, cayenne pepper, cinnamon, citron, cloves, curry-powder, flag-root, garlic, ginger, horseradish, lemon, lemon peel, mace, molasses, mustard-seed, nutmeg, onions, parsley, peach leaves, pepper, peppermint-water, rose-water, sage, summer-savory, sweet marjoram, and tomato catsup.

In addition to the use of herbs in cooking and preserving, Mrs. Child offers herbal remedies, many with a rather modern touch. She suggests sage tea as a medicine for headaches, catnip to prevent a threatened fever, succory as good for piles, and blackberries as extremely useful in cases of dysentery. She recommends a combination of lungwort, maiden-hair, hyssop, elecampane, and horehound steeped together as "an almost certain cure for a cough." Summer savory, she explains, in addition to being an excellent seasoning for soup, broth, and sausages, "relieves the colic."

Clearly, all households were expected to have a variety of alcoholic beverages readily available; the recipes call for beer, brandy, cider, claret, ginger beer, lemon-brandy, New England rum, sour beer, and wine.

The pudding section offers a great diversity of choices, from "cheap custards" to an elegant plum pudding and rich cherry or cranberry confections. There is a most intriguing recipe for potato cheese, "which is much sought after in various parts of Europe" and "has the advantage of never engendering worms, and of being preserved fresh for many years, provided it is kept in a dry place, and in well closed vessels." This is a complicated recipe and Mrs. Child admits that she does not know "whether it is worth seeking after, or not."

There are other modern touches in addition to the herbal remedies recommended. Today, we use certain woods to flavor our barbecues; Mrs. Child mentions that cobs, walnut-bark, or walnut chips, are "the best to use for smokeing, on account of the sweet taste they give the meat." She also previews what we would today call aromatherapy: "People think they must go abroad for vapor baths; but a very simple one can be made at home. Place *strong* sticks across a tub of water, at the boiling point, and sit upon them, entirely enveloped in a blanket, feet and all. The steam from the water will be a vapor-bath. Some people put herbs into the water. Steam-baths are excellent for severe colds, and for some disorders in the bowels."

Following the success of *The American Frugal Housewife*, Lydia Maria worked as a writer, publishing a variety of books and articles, including anti-slavery tracts, biographies of famous women, and three companion works to the *Frugal Housewife*: *The Little Girl's Own Book* (1831), *The Mother's Book* (1831), and *The Family Nurse* (1837).

In 1833 her life, and the life of the nation, changed when she published *An Appeal in Favor of That Class of Americans called Africans*. Her earliest biographer, the abolitionist Thomas Wentworth Higginson, who was converted to the cause because of the book, called it the "ablest" and most comprehensive antislavery book "ever printed in America." Child wrote that she was fully aware of the unpopularity of the task she had undertaken, and that she expected ridicule and censure. She was more than correct. She found herself socially ostracized, and sales of her works dwindled. The mass cancellation of subscriptions to the *Juvenile Miscellany* forced her to give up its editorship in 1834. To add insult to injury, in 1835 the Boston Athenaeum cancelled her free library privileges. (She was one of only two women to have been granted that honor.) This was a particularly serious blow because she needed the library for research purposes.

In 1841 Mrs. Child moved to New York to edit the *National Anti-Slavery Standard*, the foremost such journal in the country. She also began publishing a series of "Letters from New-York," which eventually appeared in book form (1843, and a second series in 1845). The "Letters" dealt with a wide range of social and political issues.

The remainder of her life was devoted to writing, proselytizing, and working for abolition, and, after the Civil War, to the education and advancement of the freed slaves, to universal suffrage of black men and all women, and a number of other social causes.

For half a century Lydia Maria Child was a household name in America. There was much calumny and much praise. William Lloyd Garrison, famed anti-slavery agitator hailed her as "the first woman in the republic." Senator Charles Sumner credited her with inspiring his career as an advocate of racial equality. Suffragist leader Elizabeth Cady Stanton cited Child's *History of the Condition of Women* (1835) as an invaluable resource in the fight for equality. The transcendental theologian Theodore Parker pronounced her *Progress of Religious Ideas* (1855) "*the* book of the age; and written by a *woman!*" Edgar Allen Poe praised her novel *Philothea* (1836) as "an honour to our country, and a signal triumph for our countrywomen."

Lydia Maria Child continued her writing and crusading until the end of her life. She died in Wayland, Massachusetts on October 20, 1880. A volume of her letters was published posthumously, with an introduction by John Greenleaf Whittier and an appendix by Wendell Phillips, the noted abolitionist. In his address at her funeral, Phillips declared, "She was the kind of woman one would choose to represent woman's entrance into broader life."

I have the feeling that Lydia Maria Child would consider her one and only cookery book to be a lesser contribution among her life's works, yet it painted so vivid a picture of domestic life in the first quarter of the 19th-century in America that it has become an invaluable tool for social historians and all those interested in America's past.

Once again, I wish to thank Dover for its foresight in adding this volume to their growing collection of facsimiles of classic American cookbooks.[1]

JANICE (JAN) BLUESTEIN LONGONE
The Wine and Food Library
Ann Arbor, Michigan
November 1998

1. The others are: *The First American Cookbook: A Facsimile of "American Cookery"*, 1796, Amelia Simmons [1984]; *The Virginia Housewife*, 1869, Mary Randolph [1993]; *Boston Cooking School Cook Book*, 1884, Mary J. Lincoln [1996]; *Early American Cookery: The Good Housekeeper,"* 1841, Sarah Josepha Hale [1997], *Original 1896 Boston Cooking-School Cook Book*, Fannie Farmer [1997], and *Miss Leslie's Directions for Cookery: An Unabridged Reprint of the 1851 Classic*, Eliza Leslie [1999].

Sources Consulted
and Suggested Further Reading

Baer, Helen G. *The Heart is Like Heaven: The Life of Lydia Maria Child.* Philadelphia: University of Pennsylvania Press, 1964.

Clifford, Deborah Pickman. *Crusader for Freedom: A Life of Lydia Maria Child.* Boston: Beacon Press, 1992.

Karcher, Carolyn L. *The First Woman in the Republic: A Cultural Biography of Lydia Maria Child.* Durham and London: Duke University Press, 1994.

Karcher, Carolyn, ed. *Hobomok & Other Writings on Indians by Lydia Maria Child.* New Brunswick: Rutgers University Press, 1986.

Longone, Jan. *American Cookery: The Bicentennial, 1796–1996.* Ann Arbor: The William L. Clements Library, The University of Michigan, 1996.

Longone, Janice B. and Daniel T. *American Cookbooks and Wine Books.* Ann Arbor: The Clements Library and The Wine and Food Library, 1984.

Meltzer, Milton. *Tongue of Flame: The Life of Lydia Maria Child.* New York: Thomas Y. Crowell, 1965.

Meltzer, Milton and Patricia G. Holland, eds. *Lydia Maria Child. Selected Letters, 1817–1880.* Amherst: The University of Massachusetts Press, 1982.

Mills, Bruce. *Cultural Reformations: Lydia Maria Child and the Literature of Reform.* Athens and London: The University of Georgia Press, 1994.

Osborne, William W. *Lydia Maria Child.* Boston: Twayne Publishers, 1980.

THE

AMERICAN

FRUGAL HOUSEWIFE,

DEDICATED TO THOSE

WHO ARE NOT ASHAMED OF ECONOMY.

BY MRS. CHILD,

AUTHOR OF "HOBOMOK," "THE MOTHER'S BOOK," EDITOR OF
"THE JUVENILE MISCELLANY," ETC.

A fat kitchen maketh a lean will.—*Franklin.*
"Economy is a poor man's revenue; extravagance, a rich man's ruin."

TWENTY-NINTH EDITION,
ENLARGED AND CORRECTED BY THE AUTHOR.

NEW-YORK:
SAMUEL S. & WILLIAM WOOD,
No. 261 PEARL STREET.

1844.

IT has become necessary to change the title of this work to the " *American* Frugal House-wife," because there is an *English* work of the same name, not adapted to the wants of this country.

INTRODUCTORY CHAPTER

THE true economy of housekeeping is simply the art of gathering up all the fragments, so that nothing be lost. I mean fragments of *time*, as well as *materials*. Nothing should be thrown away so long as it is possible to make any use of it, however trifling that use may be; and whatever be the size of a family, every member should be employed either in earning or saving money.

'Time is money.' For this reason, cheap as stockings are, it is good economy to knit them. Cotton and woollen yarn are both cheap; hose that are knit wear twice as long as woven ones; and they can be done at odd minutes of time, which would not be otherwise employed. Where there are children, or aged people, it is sufficient to recommend knitting, that it is an *employment*.

In this point of view, patchwork is good economy. It is indeed a foolish waste of time to tear cloth into bits for the sake of arranging it anew in fantastic figures; but a large family may be kept out of idleness, and a few shillings saved, by thus using scraps of gowns, curtains, &c.

In the country, where grain is raised, it is a good plan to teach children to prepare and braid straw for their own bonnets, and their brothers' hats.

Where turkeys and geese are kept, handsome feather fans may as well be made by the younger members of a family, as to be bought. The sooner children are taught to turn their faculties to some account, the better for them and for their parents.

In this country, we are apt to let children romp away their existence, till they get to be thirteen or fourteen. This is not well. It is not well for the purses and patience of parents; and it has a still worse effect on the morals and habits of the children. *Begin early* is the great maxim for everything in education. A child of six years old can be made useful; and should be taught to consider every day lost in which some little thing has not been done to assist others.

Children can very early be taught to take all the care of their own clothes.

They can knit garters, suspenders, and stockings; they can mak⁀ patchwork and braid straw; they can make mats for the table, and mats for the floor; they can weed the garden, and pick cranberries from the meadow, to be carried to market.

Provided brothers and sisters go together, and are not allowed to go with bad children, it is a great deal better for the boys and girls on a farm to be picking blackberries at six cents a quart, than to be wearing out their clothes in useless play. They enjoy themselves just as well; and they are earning something to buy clothes, at the same time they are tearing them.

It is wise to keep an exact account of all you expend —even of a paper of pins. This answers two purposes; it makes you more careful in spending money, and it enables your husband to judge precisely whether his family live within his income. No false pride, or foolish ambition to appear as well as others, should ever induce a person to live one cent beyond the income of which he is certain. If you have two dollars a day, let nothing but sickness induce you to spend more than nine shillings; if you have one dollar a day, do not spend but seventy-five cents; if you have half a dollar a day, be satisfied to spend forty cents.

To associate with influential and genteel people with an appearance of equality, unquestionably has its advantages; particularly where there is a family of sons and daughters just coming upon the theatre of life; but, like all other external advantages, these have their proper price, and may be bought too dearly. They who never reserve a cent of their income, with which to meet any unforeseen calamity, 'pay too dear for the whistle,' whatever temporary benefits they may derive from society. Self-denial, in proportion to the narrowness of your income, will eventually be the happiest and most respectable course for you and yours. If you are prosperous, perseverance and industry will not fail to place you in such a situation as your ambition covets; and if you are not prosperous, it will be well for your children that they have not been educated to higher hopes than they will ever realize.

If you are about to furnish a house, do not spend all your money, be it much or little. Do not let the beauty of this thing, and the cheapness of that, tempt you to buy unnecessary articles. Doctor Franklin's maxim was a wise one, 'Nothing is cheap that we do not want.' Buy merely enough to get along with at first. It is only by experience that you can tell what will be the wants of your family. If you spend all your money, you will, find you have purchased many things you do not want, and have no means left to get many things which you do want. If you have enough, and more than enough, to get everything suitable to your situation, do not think you must spend it all, merely because you happen to have it. Begin humbly. As riches increase, it is easy and pleasant to increase in hospitality and splendour; but it is always painful and inconvenient to decrease. After all, these things are view ed in their proper light by the truly judicious and respec table. Neatness, tastefulness, and good sense, may be shown in the management of a small household, and the arrangement of a little furniture, as well as upon a larger scale; and these qualities are always praised, and always treated with respect and attention. The consideration which many purchase by living beyond their income, and of course living upon others, is not worth the trouble it costs. The glare there is about this false and wicked parade is deceptive; it does not in fact procure a man valuable friends, or extensive influence. More than that, it is wrong—morally wrong, so far as the individual is concerned; and injurious beyond calculation to the inter-

ests of our country. To what are the increasing beggary
and discouraged exertions of the present period owing?
A multitude of causes have no doubt tended to increase
the evil; but the root of the whole matter is the extravagance of all classes of people. We never shall be prosperous till we make pride and vanity yield to the dictates of
honesty and prudence! We never shall be free from
embarrassment until we cease to be ashamed of industry
and economy. Let women do their share towards refor-
mation—Let their fathers and husbands see them happy
without finery; and if their husbands and fathers have
(as is often the case) a foolish pride in seeing them deco-
rated, let them gently and gradually check this feeling,
by showing that they have better and surer means of
commanding respect—Let them prove, by the exertion of
ingenuity and economy, that neatness, good taste, and gentility, are attainable without great expense.

The writer has no apology to offer for this cheap little
book of economical hints, except her deep conviction that
such a book is needed. In this case, renown is out of the
question, and ridicule is a matter of indifference.

The information conveyed is of a common kind; but
it is such as the majority of young housekeepers do not
possess, and such as they cannot obtain from cookery
books. Books of this kind have usually been written
for the wealthy : I have written for the poor. I have
said nothing about *rich* cooking; those who can afford to
be epicures will find the best of information in the ' Seventy-five Receipts.' I have attempted to teach how
money can be *saved,* not how it can be *enjoyed.* If any
persons think some of the maxims too rigidly economical,
let them inquire how the largest fortunes among us have
been made. They will find thousands and millions have
been accumulated by a scrupulous attention to sums
' infinitely more minute than sixty cents.'

In early childhood, you lay the foundation of poverty
or riches, in the habits you give your children. Teach
them to save everything,—not for their *own* use, for that
would make them selfish—but for *some* use. Teach them

to *share* everything with their playmates; but **never** allow them to *destroy* anything.

I once visited a family where the most exact economy was observed; yet nothing was mean or uncomfortable. It is the character of true economy to be as comfortable and genteel with a little, as others can be with much. In this family, when the father brought home a package, the older children would, of their own accord, put away the paper and twine neatly, instead of throwing them in the fire, or tearing them to pieces. If the little ones wanted a piece of twine to play scratch-cradle, or spin a top, there it was, in readiness; and when they threw it upon the floor, the older children had no need to be told to put it again in its place.

The other day, I heard a mechanic say, 'I have a wife and two little children; we live in a very small house; but, to save my life, I cannot spend less than twelve hundred a year.' Another replied, 'You are not economical; I spend but eight hundred.' I thought to myself,—' Neither of you pick up your twine and paper.' A third one, who was present, was silent; but after they were gone, he said, 'I keep house, and comfortably too, with a wife and children, for six hundred a year; but I suppose they would have thought me mean, if I had told them so.' I did not think him mean; it merely occurred to me that his wife and children were in the habit of picking up paper and twine.

Economy is generally despised as a low virtue, tending to make people ungenerous and selfish. This is true of avarice; but it is not so of economy. The man who is economical, is laying up for himself the permanent power of being useful and generous. He who thoughtlessly gives away ten dollars, when he owes a hundred more than he can pay, deserves no praise,—he obeys a sudden impulse, more like instinct than reason: it would be real charity to check this feeling; because the good he does may be doubtful, while the injury he does his family and creditors is certain. True economy is a careful treasurer in the service of benevolence; and where they are united respectability, prosperity and peace will follow.

ODD SCRAPS FOR THE ECONOMICAL.

IF you would avoid waste in your family, attend to the following rules, and do not despise them because they appear so unimportant : ' many a little makes a mickle.'

Look frequently to the pails, to see that nothing is thrown to the pigs which should have been in the grease-pot.

Look to the grease-pot, and see that nothing is there which might have served to nourish your own family, or a poorer one.

See that the beef and pork are always *under* brine ; and that the brine is sweet and clean.

Count towels, sheets, spoons, &c. occasionally ; that those who use them may not become careless.

See that the vegetables are neither sprouting nor decaying : if they are so, remove them to a drier place, and spread them.

Examine preserves, to see that they are not contracting mould ; and your pickles, to see that they are not growing soft and tasteless.

As far as it is possible, have bits of bread eaten up before they become hard. Spread those that are not eaten, and let them dry, to be pounded for puddings, or soaked for brewis. Brewis is made of crusts and dry pieces of bread, soaked a good while in hot milk, mashed up, and salted, and buttered like toast. Above all, do not let crusts accumulate in such quantities that they cannot be used. With proper care, there is no need of losing a particle of bread, even in the hottest weather.

Attend to all the mending in the house, once a week, if possible. Never put out sewing. If it be impossible to do it in your own family, hire some one into the house, and work with them.

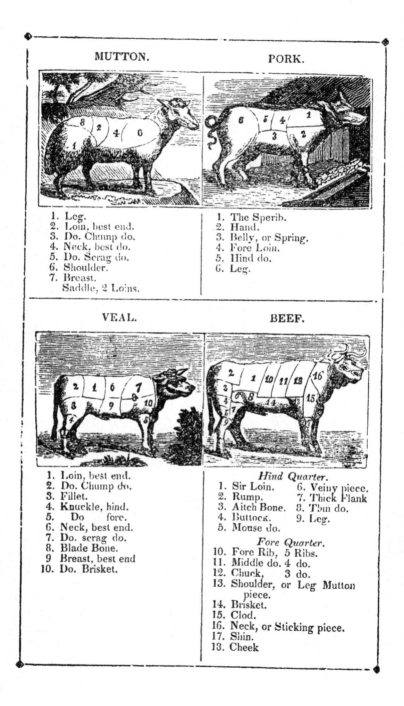

MUTTON.

1. Leg.
2. Loin, best end.
3. Do. Chump do.
4. Neck, best do.
5. Do. Scrag do.
6. Shoulder.
7. Breast.
   Saddle, 2 Loins.

PORK.

1. The Sperib.
2. Hand.
3. Belly, or Spring.
4. Fore Loin.
5. Hind do.
6. Leg.

VEAL.

1. Loin, best end.
2. Do. Chump do.
3. Fillet.
4. Knuckle, hind.
5. Do fore.
6. Neck, best end.
7. Do. scrag do.
8. Blade Bone.
9 Breast, best end
10. Do. Brisket.

BEEF.

Hind Quarter.

1. Sir Loin.	6. Veiny piece.
2. Rump.	7. Thick Flank
3. Aitch Bone.	8. Thin do.
4. Buttock.	9. Leg.
5. Mouse do.	

Fore Quarter.

10. Fore Rib, 5 Ribs.
11. Middle do. 4 do.
12. Chuck, 3 do.
13. Shoulder, or Leg Mutton piece.
14. Brisket.
15. Clod.
16. Neck, or Sticking piece.
17. Shin.
18. Cheek

Make your own bread and cake. Some people think it is just as cheap to buy of the baker and confectioner; but it is not half as cheap. True, it is more convenient; and therefore the rich are justifiable in employing them; but those who are under the necessity of being economical, should make convenience a secondary object. In the first place, confectioners make their cake richer than people of moderate income can afford to make it; in the next place, your domestic, or yourself, may just as well employ your own time, as to pay them for theirs.

When ivory-handled knives turn yellow, rub them with nice sand paper, or emery; it will take off the spots, and restore their whiteness.

When a carpet is faded, I have been told that it may be restored, in a great measure, (provided there be no grease in it,) by being dipped into strong salt and water. I never tried this; but I know that silk pocket handkerchiefs, and deep blue factory cotton will not fade, if dipped in salt and water while new.

An ox's gall will set any color,—silk, cotton, or woollen. I have seen the colors of calico, which faded at one washing, fixed by it. Where one lives near a slaughterhouse, it is worth while to buy cheap, fading goods, and set them in this way. The gall can be bought for a few cents. Get out all the liquid, and cork it up in a large phial. One large spoonful of this in a gallon of warm water is sufficient. This is likewise excellent for taking out spots from bombazine, bombazet, &c. After being washed in this, they look about as well as when new. It must be thoroughly stirred into the water, and not put upon the cloth. It is used without soap. After being washed in this, cloth which you want to *clean* should be washed in warm suds, without using soap.

Tortoise shell and horn combs last much longer for having oil rubbed into them once in a while.

Indian meal and rye meal are in danger of fermenting in summer; particularly Indian. They should be kept in a cool place, and stirred open to the air, once in a while. A large stone, put in the middle of a barrel of meal, is a good thing to keep it cool.

The covering of oil-flasks, sewed together with strong thread, and lined and bound neatly, makes useful table-mats.

A warming-pan full of coals, or a shovel of coals, held over varnished furniture, will take out white spots. Care should be taken not to hold the coals near enough to scorch; and the place should be rubbed with flannel while warm.

Spots in furniture may usually be cleansed by rubbing them quick and hard, with a flannel wet with the same thing which took out the color; if rum, wet the cloth with rum, &c. The very best restorative for defaced varnished furniture, is rotten-stone pulverized, and rubbed on with linseed oil.

Sal-volatile, or hartshorn, will restore colors taken out by acid. It may be dropped upon any garment without doing harm.

Spirits of turpentine is good to take grease-spots out of woollen clothes; to take spots of paint, &c., from mahogany furniture; and to cleanse white kid gloves. Cockroaches, and all vermin, have an aversion to spirits of turpentine.

An ounce of quicksilver, beat up with the white of two eggs, and put on with a feather, is the cleanest and surest bed-bug poison. What is left should be thrown away : it is dangerous to have it about the house. If the vermin are in your walls, fill up the cracks with ver-digris-green paint.*

Lamps will have a less disagreeable smell if you dip your wick-yarn in strong hot vinegar, and dry it.

Those who make candles will find it a great improve-ment to steep the wicks in lime-water and saltpetre, and dry them. The flame is clearer, and the tallow will not 'run.'

Britannia ware should be first rubbed gently with a wool len cloth and sweet oil; then washed in warm suds, and rubbed with soft leather and whiting. Thus treated, it will retain its beauty to the last.

---

* There are two kinds of green paint; one is of no use in destroying insects.

Eggs will keep almost any length of time in lime-water properly prepared. One pint of coarse salt, and one pint of unslacked lime, to a pailful of water. If there be too much lime, it will eat the shells from the eggs; and if there be a single egg cracked, it will spoil the whole. They should be covered with lime-water, and kept in a cold place. The yolk becomes slightly red ; but I have seen eggs, thus kept, perfectly sweet and fresh at the end of three years. The cheapest time to lay down eggs, is early in spring, and the middle and last of September. It is bad economy to buy eggs by the dozen, as you want them.

New iron should be very gradually heated at first. After it has become inured to the heat, it is not as likely to crack.

It is a good plan to put new earthen ware into cold water, and let it heat gradually, until it boils,—then cool again. Brown earthen ware, in particular, may be toughened in this way. A handful of rye, or wheat, bran, thrown in while it is boiling, will preserve the glazing, so that it will not be destroyed by acid or salt.

Clean a brass kettle, before using it for cooking, with salt and vinegar.

Skim-milk and water, with a bit of glue in it, heated scalding hot, is excellent to restore old, rusty, black Italian crape. If clapped and pulled dry, like nice muslin, it will look as well, or better, than when new.

Wash-leather gloves should be washed in clean suds, scarcely warm.

The oftener carpets are shaken, the longer they wear ; the dirt that collects under them, grinds out the threads.

Do not have carpets swept any oftener than is absolutely necessary. After dinner, sweep the crumbs into a dusting-pan with your hearth-brush ; and if you have been sewing, pick up the shreds by hand. A carpet can be kept very neat in this way ; and a broom wears it very much.

Buy your woollen yarn in quantities from some one in the country, whom you can trust. The thread-stores make profits upon it, of course.

It is not well to clean brass andirons, handles, &c. with vinegar. It makes them very clean at first; but they soon

spot and tarnish. Rotten-stone and oil are proper materials for cleaning brasses. If wiped every morning with
flannel and New England rum, they will not need to be
cleaned half as often.

If you happen to live in a house which has marble
fire-places, never wash them with suds; this destroys the
polish, in time. They should be dusted; the spots taken off with a nice oiled cloth, and then rubbed dry with
a soft rag.

Feathers should be very thoroughly dried before they
are used. For this reason they should not be packed
away in bags, when they are first plucked. They should
be laid lightly in a basket, or something of that kind, and
stirred up often. The garret is the best place to dry
them; because they will there be kept free from dirt
and moisture; and will be in no danger of being blown
away. It is well to put the parcels, which you may have
from time to time, into the oven, after you have removed
your bread, and let them stand a day.

If feather-beds smell badly, or become heavy, from
want of proper preservation of the feathers, or from old
age, empty them, and wash the feathers thoroughly in a
tub of suds; spread them in your garret to dry, and they
will be as light and as good as new.

New England rum, constantly used to wash the hair,
keeps it very clean, and free from disease, and promotes
its growth a great deal more than Macassar oil. Brandy
is very strengthening to the roots of the hair; but it has a
hot, drying tendency, which N. E. rum has not.

If you wish to preserve fine teeth, always clean them
thoroughly after you have eaten your last meal at night.

Rags should never be thrown away because they are
dirty. Mop-rags, lamp-rags, &c. should be washed, dried,
and put in the rag-bag. There is no need of expending
soap upon them : boil them out in dirty suds, after you
have done washing.

Linen rags should be carefully saved; for they are extremely useful in sickness. If they have become dirty
and worn by cleaning silver, &c., wash them, and scrape
them into lint.

After old coats, pantaloons, &c. have been cut up for boys, and are no longer capable of being converted into garments, cut them into strips, and employ the leisure moments of children, or domestics, in sewing and braiding them for door-mats.

If you are troubled to get soft water for washing, fill a tub or barrel half full of ashes, and fill it up with water, so that you may have lye whenever you want it. A gallon of strong lye put into a great kettle of hard water will make it as soft as rain water. Some people use pearlash, or potash; but this costs something, and is very apt to injure the texture of the cloth.

If you have a strip of land, do not throw away suds. Both ashes and suds are good manure for bushes and young plants.

When a white Navarino bonnet becomes soiled, rip it in pieces, and wash it with a sponge and soft water. While it is yet damp, wash it two or three times with a clean sponge dipped into a strong saffron tea, nicely strained. Repeat this till the bonnet is as dark a straw color as you wish. Press it on the wrong side with a warm iron, and it will look like a new Leghorn.

About the last of May, or the first of June, the little millers, which lay moth-eggs begin to appear. Therefore brush all your woollens, and pack them away in a dark place covered with linen. Pepper, red-cedar chips, tobacco,—indeed, almost any strong spicy smell,—is good to keep moths out of your chests and drawers. But nothing is so good as camphor. Sprinkle your woollens with camphorated spirit, and scatter pieces of camphor-gum among them, and you will never be troubled with moths. Some people buy camphor-wood trunks, for this purpose; but they are very expensive, and the gum answers just as well.

The first young leaves of the common currant-bush, gathered as soon as they put out, and dried on tin, can hardly be distinguished from green tea.

Cream of tartar, rubbed upon soiled white kid gloves, cleanses them very much.

Bottles that have been used for rose-water, should be used for nothing else ; if scalded ever so much, they will kill the spirit of what is put in them.

If you have a greater quantity of cheeses in the house than is likely to be soon used, cover them carefully with paper, fastened on with flour paste, so as to exclude the air. In this way they may be kept free from insects for years. They should be kept in a dry, cool place.

Pulverized alum possesses the property of purifying water. A large spoonful stirred into a hogshead of water will so purify it, that in a few hours the dirt will all sink to the bottom, and it will be as fresh and clear as spring water. Four gallons may be purified by a tea-spoonful.

Save vials and bottles. Apothecaries and grocers will give something for them. If the bottles are of good thick glass, they will always be useful for bottling cider or beer ; but if they are thin French glass, like claret bottles, they will not answer.

Woollens should be washed in very hot suds, and not rinsed. Lukewarm water shrinks them.

On the contrary, silk, or anything that has silk in it, should be washed in water almost cold. Hot water turns it yellow. It may be washed in suds made of nice white soap ; but no soap should be put upon it. Likewise avoid the use of hot irons in smoothing silk. Either rub the articles dry with a soft cloth, or put them between two towels, and press them with weights.

Do not let knives be dropped into hot dish-water. It is a good plan to have a large tin pot to wash them in, just high enough to wash the blades, *without wetting* the handles. Keep your castors covered with blotting-paper and green flannel. Keep your salt-spoons out of the salt, and clean them often.

Do not wrap knives and forks in woollens. Wrap them in good, strong paper. Steel is injured by lying in woollens.

If it be practicable, get a friend in the country to pro-cure you a quantity of lard, butter, and eggs, at the time they are cheapest, to be put down for winter use. You

will be likely to get them cheaper and better than in
the city market; but by all means put down your winter's
stock. Lard requires no other care than to be kept in a
dry, cool place. Butter is sweetest in September and
June; because food is then plenty, and not rendered bitter by frost. Pack your butter in a clean, scalded firkin,
cover it with strong brine, and spread a cloth all over
the top, and it will keep good until the Jews get into Grand
Isle. If you happen to have a bit of salt-petre, dissolve
it with the brine. Dairy-women say that butter comes
more easily, and has a peculiar hardness and sweetness,
if the cream is scalded and strained before it is used. The
cream should stand down cellar over night, after being
scalded, that it may get perfectly cold.

Suet and lard keep better in tin than in earthen.

Suet keeps good all the year round, if chopped and
packed down in a stone jar, covered with molasses.

Pick suet free from veins and skin, melt it in water before
a moderate fire, let it cool till it forms into a hard cake,
then wipe it dry, and put it in clean paper in linen bags.

Preserve the backs of old letters to write upon. If you
have children who are learning to write, buy coarse white
paper by the quantity, and keep it locked up, ready to be
made into writing books. It does not cost half as much as
it does to buy them at the stationer's.

Do not let coffee and tea stand in tin. Scald your
wooden ware often; and keep your tin ware dry.

When mattresses get hard and bunchy, rip them, take
the hair out, pull it thoroughly by hand, let it lie a day or
two to air, wash the tick, lay it in as light and even as
possible, and catch it down, as before. Thus prepared, they
will be as good as new.

It is poor economy to buy vinegar by the gallon. Buy
a barrel, or half a barrel, of really strong vinegar, when you
begin house-keeping. As you use it, fill the barrel with
old cider, sour beer, or wine-settlings, &c., left in pitchers,
decanters or tumblers; weak tea is likewise said to be good :
nothing is hurtful, which has a tolerable portion of spirit, or
acidity. Care must be taken not to add these things in

too large quantities, or too often : if the vinegar once gets weak, it is difficult to restore it.   If possible, it is well to keep such slops as I have mentioned in a different keg, and draw them off once in three or four weeks, in such a quantity as you think the vinegar will bear.   If by any carelessness you do weaken it, a few white beans dropped in, or white paper dipped in molasses, is said to be useful. If beer grows sour, it may be used to advantage for pancakes and fritters.   If very sour indeed, put a pint of molasses and water to it, and, two or three days after, put a half pint of vinegar ;   and in ten days it will be first rate vinegar.

Barley straw is the best for beds ; dry corn husks, slit into shreds, are far better than straw.

Straw beds are much better for being boxed at the sides ; in the same manner upholsterers prepare ticks for feathers.

Brass andirons should be cleaned, done up in papers, and put in a dry place, during the summer season. .

If you have a large family, it is well to keep white rags separate from colored ones, and cotton separate from woollen ; they bring a higher price.   Paper brings a cent a pound, and if you have plenty of room, it is well to save it.   'A penny saved is a penny got.'

Always have plenty of dish-water, and have it hot. There is no need of asking the character of a domestic, if you have ever seen her wash dishes in a little greasy water.

When molasses is used in cooking, it is a prodigious improvement to boil and skim it before you use it.   It takes out the unpleasant raw taste, and makes it almost as good as sugar.   Where molasses is used much for cooking, it is well to prepare one or two gallons in this way at a time.

In winter, always set the handle of your pump as high as possible, before you go to bed.   Except in very rigid weather, this keeps the handle from freezing.   When there is reason to apprehend extreme cold, do not forget to throw a rug or horse-blanket over your pump ; a frozen pump is a comfortless preparation for a winter's breakfast.

Never allow ashes to be taken up in wood, or put into wood.   Always have your tinder-box and lantern ready for use, in case of sudden alarm. Have important papers all together, where you can lay your hand on them at once, in case of fire.

Keep an old blanket and sheet on purpose for ironing, and on no account suffer any other to be used. Have plenty of holders always made, that your towels may not be burned out in such service.

Keep a coarse broom for the cellar stairs, wood-shed, yard, &c. No good housekeeper allows her carpet broom to be used for such things.

There should always be a heavy stone on the top of your pork, to keep it down. This stone is an excellent place to keep a bit of fresh meat in the summer, when you are afraid of its spoiling.

Have all the good bits of vegetables and meat collected after dinner, and minced before they are set away; that they may be in readiness to make a little savoury mince meat for supper or breakfast. Take the skins off your potatoes before they grow cold.

Vials, which have been used for medicine, should be put into cold ashes and water, boiled, and suffered to cool before they are rinsed.

If you live in the city, where it is always easy to procure provisions, be careful and not buy too much for your daily wants, while the weather is warm.

Never leave out your clothes-line over night; and see that your clothes-pins are all gathered into a basket.

Have plenty of crash towels in the kitchen; never let your white napkins be used there.

Soap your dirtiest clothes, and soak them in soft water over night.

Use hard soap to wash your clothes, and soft to wash your floors. Soft soap is so slippery, that it wastes a good deal in washing clothes.

Instead of covering up your glasses and pictures with muslin, cover the frames only with cheap, yellow cambric, neatly put on, and as near the color of the gilt as you can procure it. This looks better; leaves the glasses open for use, and the pictures for ornament; and is an effectual barrier to dust as well as flies.   It can easily be re-colored with saffron tea, when it is faded.

Have a bottle full cf brandy, with as large a mouth as any bottle you have, into which cut your lemon and orange peel when they are fresh and sweet.   This brandy gives a delicious flavor to all sorts of pies, puddings, and cakes. Lemon is the pleasantest spice of the two; therefore they should be kept in separate bottles.   It is a good plan to preserve rose-leaves in brandy.   The flavor is pleasanter than rose-water; and there are few people who have the utensils for distilling.   Peach leaves steeped in brandy make excellent spice for custards and puddings.

It is easy to have a supply of horse-radish all winter. Have a quantity grated, while the root is in perfection, put it in bottles, fill it with strong vinegar, and keep it corked tight.

It is thought to be a preventive to the unhealthy influence of cucumbers to cut the slices very thin, and drop each one into cold water as you cut it.   A few minutes in the water takes out a large portion of the slimy matter, so injurious to health.   They should be eaten with high seasoning.

Where sweet oil is much used, it is more economical to buy it by the bottle than by the flask.   A bottle holds more than twice as much as a flask, and it is never double the price.

If you wish to have free-stone hearths dark, wash them with soap, and wipe them with a wet cloth; some people rub in lamp-oil, once in a while, and wash the hearth faithfully afterwards.   This does very well in a large, dirty family; for the hearth looks very clean, and is not liable to show grease spots.   But if you wish to preserve the beauty of a freestone hearth, buy a quantity of free-stone powder of the stone-cutter, and rub on a portion of it wet, after you have washed your hearth in hot water.   When it is dry, brush it off, and it will look like new stone.   Bricks can be kept clean with redding stirred up in water, and put on with a brush.   Pulverized clay mixed with redding, makes a pretty rose color. Some think it is less likely to come off, if mixed with skim milk instead of water. But black lead is far handsomer than anything else for this purpose. It looks very well mixed with water, like redding; but it gives it a glossy appearance to boil the lead in soft soap, with a little water to keep it from burning. It should be put on with a brush, in the same manner as redding; it looks nice for a long time, when done in this way.

Keep a bag for odd pieces of tape and strings; they will come in use. Keep a bag or box for old buttons, so that you may know where to go when you want one.

Run the heels of stockings faithfully; and mend thin places, as well as holes. 'A stitch in time saves nine.'

Poke-root, boiled in water and mixed with a good quantity of molasses, set about the kitchen, the pantry, &c. in large deep plates, will kill cockroaches in great numbers, and finally rid the house of them. The Indians say that poke-root boiled into a soft poultice is the cure for the bite of a snake. I have heard of a fine horse saved by it.

A little salt sprinkled in starch while it is boiling, tends to prevent it from sticking; it is likewise good to stir it with a clean spermaceti candle.

A few potatoes sliced, and boiling water poured over them, makes an excellent preparation for cleansing and stiffening old rusty black silk.

Green tea is excellent to restore rusty silk. It should be boiled in iron, nearly a cup full to three quarts. The silk should not be wrung, and should be ironed damp.

Lime pulverized, sifted through coarse muslin, and stirred up tolerably thick in white of eggs, makes a strong cement for glass and china. Plaster of Paris is still better; particularly for mending broken images of the same material. It should be stirred up by the spoonful, as it is wanted.*

A bit of isinglass dissolved in gin, or boiled in spirits of wine, is said to make strong cement for broken glass, china, and sea-shells.

---

* Some think it an improvement to make whey of vinegar and milk, and heat it well up with the eggs before the lime is put in. I have heard of iron mended with it.

The lemon syrup, usually sold at fifty cents a bottle, may be made much cheaper. Those who use a great quantity of it will find it worth their while to make it. Take about a pound of Havana sugar; boil it in water down to a quart; drop in the white of an egg, to clarify it; strain it; add one quarter of an oz. of tartaric acid, or citric acid; if you do not find it sour enough, after it has stood two or three days and shaken freely, add more of the acid. A few drops of the oil of lemon improves it.

If you wish to clarify sugar and water, you are about to boil, it is well to stir in the white of one egg, while cold; if put in after it boils, the egg is apt to get hardened before it can do any good.

Those who are fond of soda powders will do well to inquire at the apothecaries for the suitable acid and alkali, and buy them by the ounce, or the pound, according to the size of their families. Experience soon teaches the right proportions; and, sweetened with a little sugar or lemon syrup, it is quite as good as what one gives five times as much for, done up in papers. The case is the same with Rochelle powders.

When the stopper of a glass decanter becomes too tight, a cloth wet with hot water and applied to the neck, will cause the glass to expand, so that the stopper may be easily removed.

Glass vessels in a cylindrical form, may be cut in two, by tying around them a worsted thread, thoroughly wet with spirits of turpentine, and then setting fire to the thread.

Court plaster is made of thin silk first dipped in dissolved isinglass and dried, then dipped several times in the white of egg and dried.

When plain tortoise-shell combs are defaced, the polish may be renewed by rubbing them with pulverized rotten-stone and oil. The rotten-stone should be sifted through muslin. It looks better to be rubbed on by the hand. The jewellers afterwards polish them by rubbing them with dry *rouge powder;* but sifted magnesia does just as well—and if the ladies had rouge, perhaps they would, *by mistake,* put it upon their cheeks, instead of their combs; and thereby spoil their complexions.

The best way to cleanse gold is, to wash it in warm suds made of delicate soap, with ten or fifteen drops of *sal-volatile* in it. This makes jewels very brilliant.

Straw carpets should be washed in salt and water, and wiped with a dry, coarse towel. They have a strong tendency to turn yellow ; and the salt prevents it. Moisture makes them decay soon ; therefore they should be kept thoroughly dry.

Rye paste is more adhesive than any other paste ; because that grain is very glutinous. It is much improved by adding a little pounded alum, while it is boiling. This makes it almost as strong as glue.

Red ants are among the worst plagues that can infest a house. A lady who had long been troubled with them, assured me she destroyed them in a few days, after the following manner. She placed a dish of cracked shag-barks (of which they are more fond than of anything else) in the closet. They soon gathered upon it in troops. She then put some corrosive sublimate in a cup; ordered the dish to be carried carefully to the fire, and all its contents brushed in ; while she swept the few that dropped upon the shelf into the cup, and, with a feather, wet all the cracks from whence they came, with corrosive sublimate. When this had been repeated four or five times, the house was effectually cleared. Too much care cannot be taken of corrosive sublimate, especially when children are about. Many dreadful accidents have happened in consequence of carelessness. Bottles which have contained it should be broken, and buried; and cups should be boiled out in ashes and water. If kept in the house, it should be hung up high, out of reach, with POISON written upon it in large letters.

The neatest way to separate wax from honey-comb is to tie the comb up in a linen or woollen bag ; place it in a kettle of cold water, and hang it over the fire. As the water heats, the wax melts, and rises to the surface, while all the impurities remain in the bag. It is well to put a few pebbles in the bag, to keep it from floating.

Honey may be separated from the comb, by placing it in the hot sun, or before the fire, with two or three colanders or sieves, each finer than the other, under it.

SOAP.

In the city, I believe, it is better to exchange ashes and grease for soap; but in the country, I am certain, it is good economy to make one's own soap. If you burn wood, you can make your own lye; but the ashes of coal is not worth much. Bore small holes in the bottom of a barrel, place four bricks around, and fill the barrel with ashes. Wet the ashes well, but not enough to drop; let it soak thus three or four days; then pour a gallon of water in every hour or two, for a day or more, and let it drop into a pail or tub beneath. Keep it dripping till the color of the lye shows the strength is exhausted. If your lye is not strong enough, you must fill your barrel with fresh ashes, and let the lye run through it. Some people take a barrel without any bottom, and lay sticks and straw across to prevent the ashes from falling through. To make a barrel of soap, it will require about five or six bushels of ashes, with at least four quarts of unslacked stone lime; if slacked, double the quantity.

When you have drawn off a part of the lye, put the lime (whether slack or not) into two or three pails of boiling water, and add it to the ashes, and let it drain through.

It is the practice of some people, in making soap, to put the lime near the bottom of the ashes when they first set it up; but the lime becomes like mortar, and the lye does not run through, so as to get the strength of it, which is very important in making soap, as it contracts the nitrous salts which collect in ashes, and prevents the soap from *coming*, (as the saying is.)   Old ashes are very apt to be impregnated with it.

Three pounds of grease should be put into a pailful of lye. The great difficulty in making soap '*come*' originates in want of judgment about the strength of the lye. One rule may be safely trusted—If your lye will bear up an egg, or a potato, so that you can see a piece of the surface as big as ninepence, it is just strong enough. If it sink below the top of the lye, it is too weak, and will never make soap; if it is buoyed up half way, the lye is too strong; and that is just as bad. A bit of quick-lime, thrown in while the lye and grease are boiling together, is of service. When the soap becomes thick and ropy, carry it down cellar in pails and empty it into a barrel.

Cold soap is less trouble, because it does not need to boil; the sun does the work of fire. The lye must be prepared and tried in the usual way. The grease must be tried out, and strained from the scraps. Two pounds of grease (instead of three) must be used to a pailful; unless the weather is very sultry, the lye should be hot when put to the grease. It should stand in the sun, and be stirred every day. If it does not begin to look like soap in the course of five or six days, add a little hot lye to it; if this does not help it, try whether it be grease that it wants. Perhaps you will think cold soap wasteful, because the grease must be strained; but if the scraps are boiled thoroughly in strong lye, the grease will all float upon the surface, and nothing be lost.

SIMPLE REMEDIES.

Cotton wool, wet with sweet oil and paregoric, relieves the ear-ache very soon.

A good quantity of old cheese is the best thing to eat, when distressed by eating too much fruit, or oppressed with any kind of food. Physicians have given it in cases of extreme danger.

Honey and milk is very good for worms; so is strong salt water; likewise powdered sage and molasses taken freely.

For a sudden attack of quincy or croup, bathe the neck with bear's grease, and pour it down the throat. A linen rag soaked in sweet oil, butter, or lard, and sprinkled with yellow Scotch snuff, is said to have performed wonderful cures in cases of croup: it should be placed where the distress is greatest. Goose-grease, or any kind of oily grease, is as good as bear's oil.

Equal parts of camphor, spirits of wine, and hartshorn, well mixed, and rubbed upon the throat, is said to be good for the croup.

Cotton wool and oil are the best things for a burn.

A poultice of wheat bran, or rye bran, and vinegar, very soon takes down the inflammation occasioned by a sprain. Brown paper, wet, is healing to a bruise. Dipped in molasses, it is said to take down inflammation.

In case of any scratch, or wound, from which the lock-jaw is apprehended, bathe the injured part freely with lye or pearl-ash and water.

A rind of pork bound upon a wound occasioned by a needle, pin, or nail, prevents the lock-jaw. It should be always applied. Spirits of turpentine is good to prevent the lock-jaw. Strong soft-soap, mixed with pulverized chalk, about as thick as batter, put, in a thin cloth or bag, upon the wound, is said to be a preventive to this dangerous disorder. The chalk should be kept moist, till the wound begins to discharge itself; when the patient will find relief.

If you happen to cut yourself slightly while cooking, bind on some fine salt: molasses is likewise good.

Flour boiled thoroughly in milk, so as to make quite a thick porridge, is good in cases of dysentery. A table-spoonful of W. I. rum, a table-spoonful of sugar-baker's molasses, and the same quantity of sweet oil, well simmered together, is likewise good for this disorder; the oil softens the harshness of the other ingredients.

Black or green tea, steeped in boiling milk, seasoned with nutmeg, and best of loaf sugar, is excellent for the dysentery. Cork burnt to charcoal, about as big as a hazel-nut, macerated, and put in a tea-spoonful of brandy, with a little loaf sugar and nutmeg, is very efficacious in cases of dysentery and cholera-morbus. If nutmeg be wanting, peppermint-water may be used. Flannel wet with brandy, powdered with Cayenne pepper, and laid upon the bowels, affords great relief in cases of extreme distress.

Dissolve as much table-salt in keen vinegar, as will ferment and work clear. When the foam is discharged, cork it up in a bottle, and put it away for use. A large spoonful of this, in a gill of boiling water, is very efficacious in cases of dysentery and colic.*

Whortleberries, commonly called huckleberries, dried, are a useful medicine for children. Made into tea, and sweetened with molasses, they are very beneficial, when the system is in a restricted state, and the digestive powers out of order.

Blackberries are extremely useful in cases of dysentery. To eat the berries is very healthy; tea made of the roots and leaves is beneficial; and a syrup made of the berries is still better. Blackberries have sometimes effected a cure when physicians despaired.

---

* Among the numerous medicines for this disease, perhaps none, after all, is better, particularly where the bowels are inflamed, than the old-fashioned one of English-mallows steeped in milk, and drank freely. Every body knows, of course, that English-mallows and marsh-mallows are different herbs.

Loaf sugar and brandy relieves a sore throat; when very bad, it is good to inhale the steam of scalding hot vinegar through the tube of a tunnel. This should be tried carefully at first, lest the throat be scalded. For children, it should be allowed to cool a little.

A stocking bound on warm from the foot, at night, is good for the sore throat.

An ointment made from the common ground-worms, which boys dig to bait fishes, rubbed on with the hand, is said to be excellent, when the sinews are drawn up by any disease or accident.

A gentleman in Missouri advertises that he had an inveterate cancer upon his nose cured by a strong potash made of the lye of the ashes of red oak bark, boiled down to the consistence of molasses. The cancer was covered with this, and, about an hour after, covered with a plaster of tar. This must be removed in a few days, and, if any protuberances remain in the wound, apply more potash to them, and the plaster again, until they entirely disappear : after which heal the wound with any common soothing salve. I never knew this to be tried.

If a wound bleeds very fast, and there is no physician at hand, cover it with the scrapings of sole-leather, scraped like coarse lint. This stops blood very soon. Always have vinegar, camphor, hartshorn, or something of that kind, in readiness, as the sudden stoppage of blood almost always makes a person faint.

Balm-of-Gilead buds bottled up in N. E. rum, make the best cure in the world for fresh cuts and wounds. Every family should have a bottle of it. The buds should be gathered in a peculiar state ; just when they are well swelled, ready to burst into leaves, and well covered with gum. They last but two or three days in this state.

Plantain and house-leek, boiled in cream, and strained before it is put away to cool, makes a very cooling, soothing ointment. Plantain leaves laid upon a wound are cooling and healing.

Half a spoonful of *citric acid*, (which may always be bought of the apothecaries,) stirred in half a tumbler of water, is excellent for the head-ache.

People in general think they must go abroad for vapor-baths; but a very simple one can be made at home. Place *strong* sticks across a tub of water, at the boiling point, and sit upon them, entirely enveloped in a blanket, feet and all. The steam from the water will be a vapor-bath. Some people put herbs into the water. Steam-baths are excellent for severe colds, and for some disorders in the bowels. They should not be taken without the advice of an experienced nurse, or physician. Great care should be taken not to renew the cold after; it would be doubly dangerous.

Boiled potatoes are said to cleanse the hands as well as common soap; they prevent *chops* in the winter season, and keep the skin soft and healthy.

Water-gruel, with three or four onions simmered in it, prepared with a lump of butter, pepper, and salt, eaten just before one goes to bed, is said to be a cure for a hoarse cold. A syrup made of horseradish-root and sugar is excellent for a cold.

Very strong salt and water, when frequently applied, has been known to cure wens.

The following poultice for the throat distemper, has been much approved in England :—The pulp of a roasted apple, mixed with an ounce of tobacco, the whole wet with spirits of wine, or any other high spirits, spread on a linen rag, and bound upon the throat at any period of the disorder.

Nothing is so good to take down swellings, as a soft poultice of stewed white beans, put on in a thin muslin bag, and renewed every hour or two.

The thin white skin, which comes from suet, is excellent to bind upon the feet for chilblains. Rubbing with Castile soap, and afterwards with honey, is likewise highly recommended. But, to cure the chilblains effectually, they must be attended to often, and for a long time.

Always apply diluted laudanum to fresh wounds.

A poultice of elder-blow tea and biscuit is good as a preventive to mortification. The approach of mortification is generally shown by the formation of blisters filled with *blood;* water blisters are not alarming.

Burnt alum held in the mouth is good for the canker.

The common dark-blue violet makes a slimy tea, which is excellent for the canker. Leaves and blossoms are both good. Those who have families should take some pains to dry these flowers.

When people have a sore mouth, from taking calomel, or any other cause, tea made of low-blackberry leaves is extremely beneficial.

Tea made of slippery elm is good for the piles, and for humors in the blood; to be drank plentifully. Winter evergreen* is considered good for all humors, particularly scrofula. Some call it rheumatism-weed; because a tea made from it is supposed to check that painful disorder.

An ointment of lard, sulphur, and cream-of-tartar, simmered together, is good for the piles.

Elixir proprietatis is a useful family medicine for all cases when the digestive powers are out of order. One ounce of saffron, one ounce of myrrh, and one ounce of aloes. Pulverize them; let the myrrh steep in half a pint of brandy, or N. E. rum, for four days; then add the saffron and aloes; let it stand in the sunshine, or in some warm place, for a fortnight; taking care to shake it well twice a day. At the end of the fortnight, fill up the bottle (a common sized one) with brandy, or N. E. rum, and let it stand a month. It costs six times as much to buy it in small quantities, as it does to make it.

The constant use of malt beer, or malt in any way, is said to be a preservative against fevers.

Black cherry-tree bark, barberry bark, mustard-seed, petty morrel-root, and horseradish, well steeped in cider, are excellent for the jaundice.

Cotton wool and oil are the best things for a burn. When children are burned, it is difficult to make them endure the application of cotton wool. I have known the inflammation of a very bad burn extracted in one night, by the constant application of brandy, vinegar, and water,

---

* This plant resembles the poisonous kill-lamb, both in the shape and the glossiness of the leaves: great care should be used to distinguish them.

mixed together. This feels cool and pleasant, and a few drops of paregoric will soon put the little sufferer to sleep. The bathing should be continued till the pain is gone.

A few drops of the oil of Cajput on cotton wool is said to be a great relief to the tooth-ache. It occasions a smart pain for a few seconds, when laid upon the defective tooth. Any apothecary will furnish it ready dropped on cotton wool, for a few cents.

A poultice made of ginger or of common chickweed, that grows about one's door in the country, has given great relief to the tooth-ache, when applied frequently to the cheek.

A spoonful of ashes stirred in cider is good to prevent sickness at the stomach. Physicians frequently order it in cases of cholera-morbus.

When a blister occasioned by a burn breaks, it is said to be a good plan to put wheat flour upon the naked flesh.

The buds of the elder bush, gathered in early spring, and simmered with new butter, or sweet lard, make a very healing and cooling ointment.

Night sweats have been cured, when more powerful remedies had failed, by fasting morning and night, and drinking cold sage tea constantly and freely.

Lard, melted and cooled five or six times in succession, by being poured each time into a fresh pail-full of water, then simmered with sliced onions, and cooled, is said, by old nurses, to make a salve, which is almost infallible in curing inflammations produced by taking cold in wounds.

Vinegar curds, made by pouring vinegar into warm milk, put on warm, and changed pretty frequently, are likewise excellent to subdue inflammation.

Chalk wet with hartshorn is a remedy for the sting of bees; so is likewise table-salt kept moist with water.

Boil castor-oil with an equal quantity of milk, sweeten it with a little sugar, stir it well, and, when cold, give it to children for drink. They will never suspect it is medicine; and will even love the taste of it.

As molasses is often given to children as a gentle physic,

it will be useful to know that West India molasses is a gentle cathartic, while sugar-baker's molasses is slightly astringent.

If a fellon or run-round appears to be coming on the finger, you can do nothing better than to soak the finger thoroughly in hot lye. It will be painful, but it will cure a disorder much more painful.

Whiskey, which has had Spanish-flies in soak, is said to be good for ring-worms; but I never knew an instance of its being tried. Unless too strong, or used in great quantities, it cannot, at least, do any harm. Washing the hands frequently in warm vinegar, is good for ring-worms.

When the toe nails have a tendency to turn in, so as to be painful, the nail should always be kept scraped *very thin*, and as near the flesh as possible. As soon as the corner of the nail can be raised up out of the flesh, it should be kept from again entering, by putting a tuft of fine lint under it.

As this book may fall into the hands of those who cannot speedily obtain a physician, it is worth while to mention what is best to be done for the bite of a rattlesnake :— Cut the flesh out, around the bite, *instantly;* that the poison may not have time to circulate in the blood. If caustic is at hand, put it upon the raw flesh; if not, the next best thing is to fill the wound with salt—renewing it occasionally. Take a dose of sweet oil and spirits of turpentine, to defend the stomach. If the whole limb swell, bathe it in salt and vinegar freely. It is well to physic the system thoroughly, before returning to usual diet.

GRUEL.

Gruel is very easily made. Have a pint of water boiling in a skillet; stir up three or four large spoonfuls of nicely sifted oat-meal, rye, or Indian, in cold water. Pour it into the skillet while the water boils. Let it boil eight or ten minutes. Throw in a large handful of raisins to boil, if the patient is well enough to bear them. When put in a bowl, add a little salt, white sugar, and nutmeg.

EGG GRUEL.

This is at once food and medicine. Some people have very great faith in its efficacy in cases of chronic dysentery. It is made thus: Boil a pint of new milk; beat four new-laid eggs to a light froth, and pour in while the milk boils; stir them together thoroughly, but do not let them boil; sweeten it with the best of loaf sugar, and grate in a whole nutmeg; add a little salt, if you like it. Drink half of it while it is warm, and the other half in two hours.

ARROW-ROOT JELLY.

Put about a pint of water in a skillet to boil; stir up a large spoonful of arrow-root powder in a cup of water; pour it into the skillet while the water is boiling; let them boil together three or four minutes. Season it with nutmeg and loaf sugar. This is very light food for an invalid. When the system is in a relaxed state, two teaspoonfuls of brandy may be put in. Milk and loaf sugar boiled, and a spoonful of fine flour, well mixed with a little cold water, poured in while the milk is boiling, is light food in cases of similar diseases.

CALF'S FOOT JELLY.

Boil four feet in a gallon of water, till it is reduced to a quart. Strain it, and let it stand, till it is quite cool. Skim off the fat, and add to the jelly one pint of wine, half a pound of sugar, the whites of six eggs, and the juice of four large lemons; boil all these materials together eight or ten minutes. Then strain into the glasses, or jars, in which you intend to keep it. Some lay a few bits of the lemon-peel at the bottom, and let it be strained upon them.

TAPIOCA JELLY.

Wash it two or three times, soak it five or six hours, simmer it in the same water with bits of fresh lemon-peel until it becomes quite clear; then put in lemon juice, wine and loaf sugar.

SAGO JELLY.

The sago should be soaked in cold water an hour, and washed thoroughly; simmered with lemon-peel and a few cloves. Add wine and loaf sugar when nearly done; and let it all boil together a few minutes.

BEEF TEA.

Beef tea, for the sick, is made by broiling a tender steak nicely, seasoning it with pepper and salt, cutting it up, and pouring water over it, not quite boiling. Put in a little water at a time, and let it stand to soak the goodness out.

WINE WHEY.

Wine whey is a cooling and safe drink in fevers. Set half a pint of sweet milk at the fire, pour in one glass of wine, and let it remain perfectly still, till it curdles; when the curds settle, strain it, and let it cool. It should not get more than blood-warm. A spoonful of rennet-water hastens the operation. Made palatable with loaf sugar and nutmeg, if the patient can bear it.

APPLE WATER.

This is given as sustenance when the stomach is too weak to bear broth, &c. It may be made thus,—Pour boiling water on roasted apples; let them stand three hours, then strain and sweeten lightly :—Or it may be made thus,—Peel and slice tart apples, add some sugar and lemon-peel; then pour some boiling water over the whole, and let it stand covered by the fire, more than an hour.

MILK PORRIDGE.

Boil new milk; stir flour thoroughly into some cold milk in a bowl, and pour it into the kettle while the milk is boiling : let it all boil six or eight minutes. Some people like it thicker than others ; I should think three large spoonfuls of flour to a quart of milk was about right. It should always be seasoned with salt ; and if the patient likes, loaf sugar and nutmeg may be put in. In cases of fever, little salt or spice should be put into any nourishment ; but in cases of dysentery, salt and nutmeg may be used freely : in such cases too, more flour should be put in porridge, and it should be boiled very thoroughly indeed.

STEWED PRUNES.

Stew them very gently in a small quantity of water, till the stones slip out. Physicians consider them safe nourishment in fevers.

VEGETABLES.

PARSNIPS should be kept down cellar, covered up in sand, entirely excluded from the air. They are good only in the spring.

Cabbages put into a hole in the ground will keep well during the winter, and be hard, fresh, and sweet, in the spring. Many farmers keep potatoes in the same way.

Onions should be kept very dry, and never carried into the cellar except in severe weather, when there is danger of their freezing. By no means let them be in the cellar after March; they will sprout and spoil. Potatoes should likewise be carefully looked to in the spring, and the sprouts broken off. The cellar is the best place for them, because they are injured by wilting ; but sprout them carefully, if you want to keep them. They never sprout but three times ; therefore, after you have sprouted them three times, they will trouble you no more.

Squashes should never be kept down cellar when it is

possible to prevent it. Dampness injures them. If intense
cold makes it necessary to put them there, bring them up
as soon as possible, and keep them in some dry, warm
place.

Cabbages need to be boiled an hour ; beets an hour
and a half. The lower part of a squash should be boiled
half an hour ; the neck pieces fifteen or twenty minutes
longer. Parsnips should boil an hour, or an hour and a
quarter, according to size. New potatoes should boil fifteen or twenty minutes ; three quarters of an hour, or an
hour, is not too much for large, old potatoes ; common-
sized ones, half an hour. In the spring, it is a good plan
to cut off a slice from the seed end of potatoes before you
cook them. The seed end is opposite to that which
grew upon the vine ; the place where the vine was broken
off may be easily distinguished. By a provision of nature,
the seed end becomes watery in the spring ; and, unless
cut off, it is apt to injure the potato. If you wish to have
potatoes mealy, do not let them stop boiling for an instant ; and
when they are done, turn the water off, and let them steam
for ten or twelve minutes over the fire. See they don't
stay long enough to burn to the kettle. In Canada, they
cut the skin all off, and put them in pans, to be cooked
over a stove, by steam. Those who have eaten them, say
they are mealy and white, looking like large snow-balls
when brought upon the table.

Potatoes boiled and mashed while hot, are good to use
in making short cakes and puddings ; they save flour, and
less shortening is necessary.

It is said that a bit of unslacked lime, about as big as a
robin's egg, thrown among old, watery potatoes, while they
are boiling, will tend to make them mealy. I never saw
the experiment tried.

Asparagus should be boiled fifteen or twenty minutes ;
half an hour, if old.

Green peas should be boiled from twenty minutes to
sixty, according to their age ; string beans the same. Corn
should be boiled from twenty minutes to forty, according
to age ; dandelions half an hour, or three quarters, ac-

cording to age. Dandelions are very much improved by cultivation. If cut off, without injuring the root, they will spring up again, fresh and tender, till late in the season.

Beet-tops should be boiled twenty minutes; and spinage three or four minutes. Put in no green vegetables till the water boils, if you would keep all their sweetness.

When green peas have become old and yellow, they may be made tender and green by sprinkling in a pinch or two of pearlash, while they are boiling. Pearlash has the same effect upon all summer vegetables, rendered tough by being too old. If your well-water is very hard, it is always an advantage to use a little pearlash in cooking.

Tomatoes should be skinned by pouring boiling water over them. After they are skinned, they should be stewed half an hour, in tin, with a little salt, a small bit of butter, and a spoonful of water, to keep them from burning. This is a delicious vegetable. It is easily cultivated, and yields a most abundant crop. Some people pluck them green, and pickle them.

The best sort of catsup is made from tomatoes. The vegetables should be squeezed up in the hand, salt put to them, and set by for twenty-four hours. After being passed through a sieve, cloves, allspice, pepper, mace, garlic, and whole mustard-seed should be added. It should be boiled down one third, and bottled after it is cool. No liquid is necessary, as the tomatoes are very juicy. A good deal of salt and spice is necessary to keep the catsup well. It is delicious with roast meat; and a cupful adds much to the richness of soup and chowder. The garlic should be taken out before it is bottled.

Celery should be kept in the cellar, the roots covered with tan, to keep them moist.

Green squashes that are turning yellow, and striped squashes, are more uniformly sweet and mealy than any other kind.

If the tops of lettuce be cut off when it is becoming too old for use, it will grow up again fresh and tender, and may thus be kept good through the summer.

It is a good plan to boil onions in milk and water; it diminishes the strong taste of that vegetable. It is an excellent way of serving up onions, to chop them after they are boiled, and put them in a stewpan, with a little milk, butter, salt, and pepper, and let them stew about fifteen minutes. This gives them a fine flavor, and they can be served up very hot.

HERBS.

ALL herbs should be carefully kept from the air. Herb tea, to do any good, should be made *very strong*.

Herbs should be gathered while in blossom. If left till they have gone to seed, the strength goes into the seed. Those who have a little patch of ground, will do well to raise the most important herbs; and those who have not, will do well to get them in quantities from some friend in the country; for apothecaries make very great profit upon them.

Sage is very useful both as a medicine, for the headache—when made into tea—and for all kinds of stuffing, when dried and rubbed into powder. It should be kept tight from the air.

Summer-savory is excellent to season soup, broth, and sausages. As a medicine, it relieves the cholic. Pennyroyal and tansy are good for the same medicinal purpose.

Green wormwood bruised is excellent for a fresh wound of any kind. In winter, when wormwood is dry, it is necessary to soften it in warm vinegar, or spirit, before it is bruised, and applied to the wound.

Hyssop tea is good for sudden colds, and disorders on the lungs. It is necessary to be very careful about exposure after taking it; it is peculiarly opening to the pores.

Tea made of colt's-foot and flax-seed, sweetened with honey, is a cure for inveterate coughs. Consumptions have been prevented by it. It should be drank when going to bed; though it does good to drink it at any time. Hoarhound is useful in consumptive complaints.

Motherwort tea is very quieting to the nerves. Students, and people troubled with wakefulness, find it useful.

Thoroughwort is excellent for dyspepsy, and every disorder occasioned by indigestion. If the stomach be foul, it operates like a gentle emetic.

Sweet-balm tea is cooling when one is in a feverish state.

Catnip, particularly the blossoms, made into tea, is good to prevent a threatened fever. It produces a fine perspiration. It should be taken in bed, and the patient kept warm.

Housekeepers should always dry leaves of the burdock and horseradish. Burdocks warmed in vinegar, with the hard, stalky parts cut out, are very soothing, applied to the feet; they produce a sweet and gentle perspiration. Horseradish is more powerful. It is excellent in cases of the ague, placed on the part affected. Warmed in vinegar, and clapped.

Succory is a very valuable herb. The tea, sweetened with molasses, is good for the piles. It is a gentle and healthy physic, a preventive of dyspepsy, humors, inflammation, and all the evils resulting from a restricted state of the system.

Elder-blow tea has a similar effect. It is cool and soothing, and peculiarly efficacious either for babes or grown people, when the digestive powers are out of order.

Lungwort, maiden-hair, hyssop, elecampane and hoarhound steeped together, is an almost certain cure for a cough. A wine-glass full to be taken when going to bed.

Few people know how to keep the flavor of sweet-marjoram; the best of all herbs for broth and stuffing. It should be gathered in bud or blossom, and dried in a tinkitchen at a moderate distance from the fire; when dry, it should be immediately rubbed, sifted, and corked up in a bottle carefully.

English-mallows steeped in milk is good for the dysentery.

CHEAP DYE-STUFFS.

A few general rules are necessary to be observed in coloring. The materials should be perfectly clean; soap should be rinsed out in soft water; the article should be entirely wetted, or it will spot; light colors should be steeped in brass, tin, or earthen; and if set at all, should be set with alum. Dark colors should be boiled in iron, and set with copperas. Too much copperas rots the thread.

The apothecaries and hatters keep a compound of vitriol and indigo, commonly called ' blue composition.' An ounce vial full may be bought for nine-pence. It colors a fine blue. It is an economical plan to use it for old silk linings, ribbons, &c. The original color should be boiled out, and the material thoroughly rinsed in soft water, so that no soap may remain in it; for soap ruins the dye. Twelve or sixteen drops of the blue composition, poured into a quart bowl full of warm soft water, stirred, (and strained, if any settlings are perceptible,) will color a great many articles. If you wish a deep blue, pour in more of the compound. Cotton must not be colored; the vitriol destroys it; if the material you wish to color has cotton threads in it, it will be ruined. After the things are thoroughly dried, they should be washed in cool suds, and dried again; this prevents any bad effects from the vitriol; if shut up from the air without being washed, there is danger of the texture being destroyed. If you wish to color green, have your cloth free as possible from the old color, clean, and rinsed, and, in the first place, color it a deep yellow. Fustic boiled in soft water makes the strongest and brightest yellow dye; but saffron, barberry bush, peach leaves, or onion skins, will answer pretty well. Next take a bowl full of strong yellow dye, and pour in a great spoonful or more of the blue composition. Stir it up well with a clean stick, and dip the articles you have already colored yellow into it, and they will take a lively grass green. This is a good plan for old bombazet curtains, dessert cloths, old flannel for covering a desk, &c; it is likewise a handsome color for ribbons.

Balm blossoms, steeped in water, color a pretty rose-color. This answers very well for the linings of children's bonnets, for ribbons, &c. It fades in the course of one season; but it is very little trouble to recolor with it. It merely requires to be steeped and strained. Perhaps a small piece of alum might serve to set the color, in some degree. In earthen or tin.

Saffron, steeped in earthen and strained, colors a fine straw color. It makes a delicate or deep shade according to the strength of the tea. The dry outside skins of onions, steeped in scalding water and strained, color a yellow very much like 'bird of paradise' color. Peach leaves, or bark scraped from the barberry bush, colors a common bright yellow. In all these cases, a little piece of alum does no harm, and may help to fix the color. Ribbons, gauze handkerchiefs, &c. are colored well in this way, especially if they be stiffened by a bit of gum-Arabic, dropped in while the stuff is steeping.

The purple paper, which comes on loaf sugar, boiled in cider, or vinegar, with a small bit of alum, makes a fine purple slate color. Done in iron.

White maple bark makes a good light-brown slate color. This should be boiled in water, set with alum. The color is reckoned better when boiled in brass, instead of iron.

The purple slate and the brown slate are suitable colors for stockings; and it is an economical plan, after they have been mended and cut down, so that they will no longer look decent, to color old stockings, and make them up for children.

A pailful of lye, with a piece of copperas half as big as a hen's egg boiled in it, will color a fine nankin color, which will never wash out. This is very useful for the linings of bed-quilts, comforters, &c. Old faded gowns, colored in this way, may be made into good petticoats. Cheap cotton cloth may be colored to advantage for petticoats, and pelisses for little girls.

A very beautiful nankin color may likewise be obtained from birch-bark, set with alum. The bark should be covered with water, and boiled thoroughly in brass or tin. A bit of alum half as big as a hen's egg is sufficient. If copperas be used instead of alum, slate color will be produced.

Tea-grounds boiled in iron, and set with copperas, make a very good slate color.

Log-wood and cider, in iron, set with copperas, makes a good black. Rusty nails, or any rusty iron, boiled in vinegar, with a small bit of copperas, makes a good black, —black ink-powder done in the same way answers the same purpose.

MEAT CORNED, OR SALTED, HAMS, &c.

WHEN you merely want to corn meat, you have nothing to do but to rub in salt plentifully, and let it set in the cellar a day or two. If you have provided more meat than you can use while it is good, it is well to corn it in season to save it. In summer, it will not keep well more than a day and a half; if you are compelled to keep it longer, be sure and rub in more salt, and keep it carefully covered from cellar-flies. In winter, there is no difficulty in keeping a piece of corned beef a fortnight or more. Some people corn meat by throwing it into their beef barrel for a few days; but this method does not make it so sweet. A little salt-petre rubbed in before you apply the common salt, makes the meat tender; but in summer it is not well to use it, because it prevents the other salt from impregnating; and the meat does not keep as well.

If you wish to salt fat pork, scald coarse salt in water and skim it, till the salt will no longer melt in the water. Pack your pork down in tight layers; salt every layer; when the brine is cool, cover the pork with it, and keep a heavy stone on the top to keep the pork under brine. Look to it once in a while, for the first few weeks, and if the salt has all melted, throw in more. This brine, scalded and skimmed every time it is used, will continue good twenty years. The rind of the pork should be packed towards the edge of the barrel.

It is good economy to salt your own beef as well as pork. Six pounds of coarse salt, eight ounces of brown sugar, a pint of molasses, and eight ounces of salt-petre, are enough to boil in four gallons of water. Skim it clean while boiling. Put it to the beef cold; have enough to cover it; and be careful your beef never floats on the top. If it does not smell perfectly sweet, throw in more salt; if a scum rises upon it, scald and skim it again, and pour it on the beef when cold.

Legs of mutton are very good, cured in the same way as ham. Six pounds of salt, eight ounces of salt-petre, and five pints of molasses, will make pickle enough for one hundred weight. Small legs should be kept in pickle twelve or fifteen days; if large, four or five weeks are not too much. They should be hung up a day or two to dry, before they are smoked. Lay them in the oven, on crossed sticks, and make a fire at the entrance. Cobs, walnut-bark, or walnut-chips, are the best to use for smoking, on account of the sweet taste they give the meat. The smallest pieces should be smoked forty-eight hours, and large legs four or five days. Some people prefer the mutton boiled as soon as it is taken from the pickle, before it is smoked; others hang it up till it gets dry thoroughly, and eat it in thin slices, like hung beef. When legs of meat are put in pickle, the thickest part of the leg should be placed uppermost, that is, standing upright, the same as the creature stood when living. The same rule should be observed when they are hung up to dry; it is essential in order to keep in the juices of the meat. Meat should be turned over once or twice during the process of smoking.

The old-fashioned way for curing hams is to rub them with salt very thoroughly, and let them lay twenty-four hours. To each ham allow two ounces of salt-petre, one quart of common salt and one quart of molasses. First baste them with molasses; next rub in the salt-petre : and,

last of all, the common salt. They must be carefully turned and rubbed every day for six weeks; then hang them
in a chimney, or smoke-house, four weeks.

They should be well covered up in paper bags, and put
in a chest, or barrel, with layers of ashes, or charcoal, between. When you take out a ham to cut for use, be sure
and put it away in a dark place, well covered up; especially in summer.

Some very experienced epicures and cooks, think the
old-fashioned way of preparing bacon is troublesome and
useless. They say that legs of pork placed upright in pickle, for four or five weeks, are just as nice as those rubbed
with so much care. The pickle for pork and hung beef,
should be stronger than for legs of mutton. Eight
pounds of salt, ten ounces of salt-petre and five pints of
molasses is enough for one hundred weight of meat; water enough to cover the meat well—probably, four or five
gallons. Any one can prepare bacon, or dried beef, very
easily, in a common oven, according to the above directions. The same pickle that answers for bacon is proper
for neat's tongues. Pigs' tongues are very nice, prepared
in the same way as neat's tongues; an abundance of them
are sold for rein-deer's tongues, and, under that name, considered a wonderful luxury.

Neat's tongue should be boiled full three hours. If it
has been in salt long, it is well to soak it over night in cold
water. Put it in to boil when the water is cold. If you
boil it in a small pot, it is well to change the water, when
it has boiled an hour and a half; the fresh water should
boil before the half-cooked tongue is put in again. It is
nicer for being kept in a cool place a day or two after being
boiled. Nearly the same rules apply to salt beef. A six
pound piece of corned beef should boil full three hours;
and salt beef should be boiled four hours.

The salter meat is, the longer it should be boiled. If
very salt, it is well to put it in soak over night; change the
water while cooking; and observe the same rules as in
boiling tongue. If it is intended to be eaten when cold, it
is a good plan to put it between clean boards, and press it

down with heavy weights for a day or two. A small leg of bacon should be boiled three hours; ten pounds four hours; twelve pounds five hours. All meat should boil moderately; furious boiling injures the flavor.

Buffalo's tongue should soak a day and a night, and boil as much as six hours.

CHOICE OF MEAT.

IF people wish to be economical, they should take some pains to ascertain what are the cheapest pieces of meat to buy; not merely those which are cheapest in price, but those which go farthest when cooked. That part of mutton called the rack, which consists of the neck, and a few of the rib bones below, is cheap food. It is not more than four or five cents a pound; and four pounds will make a dinner for six people. The neck, cut into pieces, and boiled slowly an hour and a quarter, in little more than water enough to cover it, makes very nice broth. A great spoonful of rice should be washed and thrown in with the meat. About twenty minutes before it is done, put in a little thickening, and season with salt, pepper, and sifted summer-savory, or sage. The bones below the neck, broiled, make a good mutton chop. If your family be small, a rack of mutton will make you two dinners,—broth once, and mutton chop with a few slices of salt pork, for another; if your family consist of six or seven, you can have two dishes for a dinner. If you boil the whole rack for broth, there will be some left for mince meat.

Liver is usually much despised; but when well cooked, it is very palatable; and it is the cheapest of all animal food. Veal liver is by some considered the best. Veal liver is usually two cents a pound; beef liver is one cent. After you have fried a few slices of salt pork, put the liver in while the fat is very hot, and cook it through thorough-

ly. If you doubt whether it be done, cut into a slice, and
see whether it has turned entirely brown, without any red
stripe in the middle. Season it with pepper and salt, and
butter, if you live on a farm, and have butter in plenty.
It should not be cooked on furiously hot coals, as it is very
apt to scorch. Sprinkle in a little flour, stir it, and pour
in boiling water to make gravy, just as you would for fried
meat. Some think liver is better dipped in sifted Indian
meal before it is fried. It is good broiled and buttered
like a steak. It should be cut into slices about as thick as
are cut for steaks.

The heart, liver, &c. of a pig is good fried ; so is that of
a lamb. The latter is commonly called lamb-fry ; and a
dinner may be bought for six or eight cents. Be sure and
ask for the sweet-bread ; for butchers are extremely apt to
reserve it for their own use ; and therefore lamb-fry is almost always sold without it. Fry five or six slices of salt
pork ; after it is taken out, put in your lamb-fry while the
fat is hot. Do it thoroughly ; but be careful the fire is not
too furious, as it is apt to scorch. Take a large handful of
parsley, see that it is washed clean, cut it up pretty fine ;
then pour a little boiling water into the fat in which your
dinner has been fried, and let the parsley cook in it a minute or two ; then take it out in a spoon, and lay it over
your slices of meat. Some people, who like thick gravies,
shake in a little flour into the spider, before pouring in the
boiling water.

Bones from which roasting pieces have been cut, may
be bought in the market for ten or twelve cents, from which
a very rich soup may be made, besides skimming off fat
for shortening. If the bones left from the rump be bought,
they will be found full of marrow, and will give more than a
pint of good shortening, without injuring the richness of the
soup. The richest piece of beef for a soup is the leg and
the shin of beef ; the leg is on the hind quarter, and the shin
is on the fore quarter. The leg rand, that is, the thick
part of the leg above the bony parts, is very nice for mince
pies. Some people have an objection to these parts of
beef, thinking they must be stringy ; but, if boiled *very ten-*

der, the sinews are not perceived, and add, in fact, to the richness of a soup.

The thick part of a thin flank is the most profitable part in the whole ox to buy. It is not so handsome in appearance as some other pieces, but it is thick meat, with very little bone, and is usually two cents less in the pound tnan more fashionable pieces. It is good for roasting, and particularly for corning and salting. The navel end of the brisket is one of the best pieces for salting or corning, and is very good for roasting.

The rattle rand is the very best piece for corning, or salting.

A bullock's heart is very profitable to use as a steak. Broiled just like beef. There are usually five pounds in a heart, and it can be bought for twenty-five cents. Some people stuff and roast it.

The chuck, between the neck and the shoulder, is a very good piece for roasting,—for steaks, or for salting. Indeed, it is good for almost anything; and it is cheap, being from four to five cents a pound.

The richest, tenderest, and most delicate piece of beef for roasting, or for steak, is the rump and the last cut of the sirloin. It is peculiarly appropriate for an invalid, as it is lighter food than any other beef.

But if economy be consulted instead of luxury, the round will be bought in preference to the rump. It is heartier food, and, of course, less can be eaten; and it is cheaper in price.

The shoulder of veal is the most economical for roasting or boiling. It is always cheap, let veal bear what price it may. Two dinners may be made from it; the shoulder roasted, and the knuckle cut off to be boiled with a bit of pork and greens, or to be made into soup.

The breast of veal is a favorite piece, and is sold lugh.

The hind-quarter of veal and the loin make two good roasting pieces. The leg is usually stuffed. The line has the kidney upon it; the fore-quarter has the brisket on it. This is a sweet and delicate morsel; for this reason some people prefer the fore-quarter to any other part.

Always buy a shoulder of pork for economy, for roasting, or corning to boil. Cut off the leg to be boiled. Many people buy the upper part of the spare-rib of pork, thinking it the most genteel; but the lower part of the spare-rib toward the neck is much more sweet and juicy, and there is more meat in proportion to the bone.

The breast, or shoulder, of mutton are both nice, either for roasting, boiling or broth. The breast is richer than the shoulder. It is more economical to buy a fore-quarter of mutton than a hind-quarter; there is usually two cents difference per pound. The neck of fat mutton makes a good steak for broiling.

Lamb brings the same price, either fore-quarter or hind-quarter; therefore it is more profitable to buy a hind-quarter than a fore-quarter; especially as its own fat will cook it, and there is no need of pork or butter in addition. Either part is good for roasting or boiling. The loin of lamb is suitable for roasting, and is the most profitable for a small family. The leg is more suitable for boiling than for anything else; the shoulder and breast are peculiarly suitable for broth.

The part that in lamb is called the loin, in mutton is called the chop. Mutton chop is considered very good for broiling.

Pig's head is a profitable thing to buy. It is despised, because it is cheap; but when well cooked it is delicious. Well cleaned, the tip of the snout chopped off, and put in brine a week, it is very good for boiling: the cheeks, in particular, are very sweet; they are better than any other pieces of pork to bake with beans. The head is likewise very good baked about an hour and a half. It tastes like roast pork, and yields abundance of sweet fat, for shortening.

COMMON COOKING.

It is necessary to be very careful of fresh meat in the summer season. The moment it is brought into the house, it should be carefully covered from the flies, and put in the coldest place in the cellar. If it consist of pie'ces, they should be spread out separate from each other, on a large dish, and covered. If you are not to cook it soon, it is well to sprinkle salt on it. The kidney, and fat flabby parts, should be raised up above the lean, by a skewer, or stick, and a little salt strewn in. If you have to keep it over night, it should be looked to the last thing when you go to bed ; and if there is danger, it should be scalded.

VEAL.

Veal should boil about an hour, if a neck-piece; if the meat comes from a thicker, more solid part, it should boil longer. No directions about these things will supply the place of judgment and experience. Both mutton and veal are better for being boiled with a small piece of salt pork. Veal broth is very good.

Veal soup should be slowly stewed for two hours. Seasoned the same as above. Some people like a little sifted summer-savory.

Six or seven pounds of veal will roast in an hour and a half.

Fried veal is better for being dipped in white of egg, and rolled in nicely pounded crumbs of bread, before it is cooked. One egg is enough for a common dinner.

CALF'S HEAD.

Calf's head should be cleansed with very great care ; particularly the lights. The head, the heart, and the lights should boil full two hours ; the liver should be boiled only one hour. It is better to leave the wind-pipe on, for if it hangs out of the pot while the head is cooking, all the froth will escape through it. The brains, after being thoroughly washed, should be put in a little bag; with one pounded cracker, or as much crumbled bread, seasoned with sifted sage, and tied up and boiled one hour. After the brains are boiled, they should be well broken up with a knife, and peppered, salted, and buttered. They should be put upon the table in a bowl by themselves. Boiling water, thickened with flour and water, with butter melted in it, is the proper sauce; some people love vinegar and pepper mixed with the melted butter; but all are not fond of it; and it is easy for each one to add it for themselves.

BEEF.

Beef soup should be stewed four hours over a slow fire. Just water enough to keep the meat covered. If you have any bones left of roast meat, &c. it is a good plan to boil them with the meat, and take them out half an hour before the soup is done. A pint of flour and water, with salt, pepper, twelve or sixteen onions, should be put in twenty minutes before the soup is done. Be careful and not throw in salt and pepper too plentifully; it is easy to add to it, and not easy to diminish. A lemon, cut up and put in half an hour before it is done, adds to the flavor. If you have tomato catsup in the house, a cupful will make soup rich. Some people put in crackers; some thin slices of crust, made nearly as short as common short-cake; and some stir up two or three eggs with milk and flour, and drop it in with a spoon.

A quarter of an hour to each pound of beef is considered a good rule for roasting; but this is too much when the bone is large, and the meat thin. Six pounds of the rump should roast six quarters of an hour; but bony pieces less It should be done before a quick fire.

The quicker beef-steak can be broiled the better. Seasoned after it is taken from the gridiron.

ALAMODE BEEF.

Tie up a round of beef so as to keep it in shape; make a stuffing of grated bread, suet, sweet herbs, quarter of an ounce of nutmeg, a few cloves pounded, yolk of an egg. Cut holes in the beef, and put in the stuffing, leaving about half the stuffing to be made into balls. Tie the beef up in a cloth, just cover it with water, let it boil an hour and a half; then turn it, and let it boil an hour and a half more; then turn out the liquor, and put some skewers across the bottom of the pot, and lay the beef upon it, to brown; turn it that it may brown on both sides. Put a pint of claret, and some allspice and cloves, into the liquor, and boil some balls made of the stuffing in it.

MUTTON AND LAMB.

Six or seven pounds of mutton will roast in an hour and a half. Lamb one hour. Mutton is apt to taste strong; this may be helped by soaking the meat in a little salt and water, for an hour before cooking. However, unless meat is very sweet, it is best to corn it, and boil it. Fresh meat should never be put in to cook till the water boils; and it should be boiled in as little water as possible; otherwise the flavor is injured. Mutton enough for a family of five or six should boil an hour and a half. A leg of lamb should boil an hour, or little more than an hour, perhaps. Put a little thickening into boiling water; strain it nicely; and put sweet butter in it for sauce. If your family like broth, throw in some clear rice when you put in the meat. The rice should be in proportion to the quantity of broth you mean to make. A large table spoonful is enough for three pints of water. Seasoned with a very little pepper and salt. Summer-savory, or sage, rubbed through a sieve, thrown in.

PORK.

Fresh pork should be cooked more than any other meat. A thick shoulder piece should be roasted full two hours and a half; and other pieces less in proportion. The slight sickness occasioned by eating roasted pork may be prevented by soaking it in salt and water the night before you cook it.   If called to prepare it on short notice, it will answer to baste it with weak brine while roasting; and then turn the brine off, and throw it away.

ROAST PIG.

Strew fine salt over it an hour before it is put down. It should not be cut entirely open; fill it up plump with thick slices of buttered bread, salt, sweet-marjoram and sage. Spit it with the head next the point of the spit; take off the joints of the leg, and boil them with the liver, with a little whole pepper, allspice, and salt, for gravy sauce. The upper part of the legs must be braced down with skewers. Shake on flour. Put a little water in the dripping-pan, and stir it often. When the eyes drop out, the pig is half done. When it is nearly done, baste it with butter. Cut off the head, split it open between the eyes. Take out the brains, and chop them fine with the liver and some sweet-marjoram and sage; put this into melted butter, and when it has boiled a few minutes, add it to the gravy in the dripping-pan. When your pig is cut open, lay it with the back to the edge of the dish; half a head to be placed at each end. A good sized pig needs to be roasted three hours.

SAUSAGES.

Three tea-spoons of powdered sage, one and a half of salt, and one of pepper, to a pound of meat, is good seasoning for sausages.

MINCE MEAT.

There is a great difference in preparing mince meat. Some make it a coarse, unsavory dish; and others make it nice and palatable. No economical house-keeper will despise it; for broken bits of meat and vegetables cannot so well be disposed of in any other way. If you wish to have it nice, mash your vegetables fine, and chop your meat very fine. Warm it with what remains of sweet gravy, or roast-meat drippings, you may happen to have. Two or three apples, pared, cored, sliced, and fried, to mix with it, is an improvement. Some like a little sifted sage sprinkled in.

It is generally considered nicer to chop your meat fine, warm it in gravy, season it, and lay it upon a large slice of toasted bread to be brought upon the table without being mixed with potatoes ; but if you have cold vegetables, use them.

BEANS AND PEAS.

Baked beans are a very simple dish, yet few cook them well. They should be put in cold water, and hung over the fire, the night before they are baked. In the morning, they should be put in a colander, and rinsed two or three times ; then again placed in a kettle, with the pork you intend to bake, covered with water, and kept scalding hot, an hour or more. A pound of pork is quite enough for a quart of beans, and that is a large dinner for a common family. The rind of the pork should be slashed. Pieces of pork alternately fat and lean, are the most suitable ; the cheeks are the best. A little pepper sprinkled among the beans, when they are placed in the bean-pot, will render them less unhealthy. They should be just covered with water, when put into the oven ; and the pork should be sunk a little below the surface of the beans. Bake three or four hours.

Stewed beans are prepared in the same way. The only difference is, they are not taken out of the scalding water, but are allowed to stew in more water, with a piece of pork and a little pepper, three hours or more.

Dried peas need not be soaked over night. They should be stewed slowly four or five hours in considerable water, with a piece of pork. The older beans and peas are, the longer they should cook. Indeed, this is the case with all vegetables.

SOUSE.

Pigs' feet, ears, &c., should be cleaned after being soaked in water not very hot; the hoofs will then come off easily with a sharp knife; the hard, rough places should be cut off; they should be thoroughly singed, and then boiled as much as four or five hours, until they are too tender to be taken out with a fork. When taken from the boiling water, it should be put into cold water. After it is packed down tight, boil the jelly-like liquor in which it was cooked with an equal quantity of vinegar; salt as you think fit, and cloves, allspice, and cinnamon, at the rate of a quarter of a pound to one hundred weight: to be poured on scalding hot.

TRIPE.

Tripe should be kept in cold water, or it will become too dry for cooking. The water in which it is kept should be changed more or less frequently, according to the warmth of the weather. Broiled like a steak, buttered, peppered, &c. Some people like it prepared like souse.

GRAVY.

Most people put a half a pint of flour and water into their tin-kitchen, when they set meat down to roast. This does very well; but gravy is better flavored, and looks darker, to shake flour and salt upon the meat; let it brown thoroughly, put flour and salt on again, and then baste the meat with about half a pint of hot water (or more, according to the gravy you want.) When the meat is about done, pour these drippings into a skillet, and let it boil. If it is not thick enough, shake in a little flour; but be sure to let it boil, and be well stirred, after the flour is in. If you fear it will be too greasy, take off a cupful of the fat before you boil. The fat of beef, pork, turkeys and geese is as good for shortening as lard. Salt gravy to your taste. If you are very particular about dark gravies, keep your dredging-box full of scorched flour for that purpose.

POULTRY.

There are various ways of deciding about the age of poultry.

If the bottom of the breast bone, which extends down between the legs, is soft, and gives easily, it is a sign of youth ; if stiff, the poultry is old.

If young, the legs are lighter, and the feet do not look so hard, stiff, and worn.

There is more deception in geese than in any other kind of poultry. The above remarks are applied to them ; but there are other signs more infallible. In a young goose, the cavity under the wings is very tender ; it is a bad sign if you cannot, with very little trouble, push your finger directly into the flesh. There is another means by which you may decide whether a goose be tender, if it be frozen or not. Pass the head of a pin along the breast, or sides, and if the goose be young, the skin will rip, like fine paper under a knife.

Something may be judged concerning the age of a goose by the thickness of the web between the toes. When young, this is tender and transparent ; it grows coarser and harder with time.

In broiling chickens, it is difficult to do the inside of the thickest pieces without scorching the outside. It is a good plan to parboil them about ten minutes in a spider or skillet, covered close to keep the steam in ; then put them upon the gridiron, broil and butter. It is a good plan to cover them with a plate, while on the gridiron. They may be basted with a very little of the water in which they were broiled ; and if you have company who like melted butter to pour upon the chicken, the remainder of the liquor will be good use for that purpose.

An hour is enough for common sized chickens to roast. A smart fire is better than a slow one ; but they must be tended closely. Slices of bread, buttered, salted, and peppered, put into the stomach (not the crop) are excellent.

Chickens should boil about an hour. If old, they should

boil longer. In as little water as will cook them. Chicken-broth made like mutton-broth.

FRICASSEED CHICKEN, BROWN.

Singe the chickens; cut them in pieces; pepper, salt, and flour them; fry them in fresh butter, till they are very brown: take the chickens out, and make a good gravy, into which put sweet herbs (marjoram or sage) according to your taste; if necessary, add pepper and salt; butter and flour must be used in making the gravy, in such quantities as to suit yourself for thickness and richness. After this is all prepared, the chicken must be stewed in it, for half an hour, closely covered. A pint of gravy is about enough for two chickens; I should think a piece of butter about as big as a walnut, and a table-spoonful of flour, would be enough for the gravy. The herbs should, of course, be pounded and sifted. Some, who love onions, slice two or three, and brown them with the chicken. Some slice a half lemon, and stew with the chicken. Some add tomatoes catsup.

FRICASSEED CHICKEN, WHITE.

The chickens are cut to pieces, and covered with warm water, to draw out the blood. Then put into a stew-pan, with three quarters of a pint of water, or veal broth, salt, pepper, flour, butter, mace, sweet herbs pounded and sifted; boil it half an hour. If it is too fat, skim it a little. Just before it is done, mix the yolk of two eggs with a gill of cream, grate in a little nutmeg, stir it up till it is thick and smooth, squeeze in half a lemon. If you like onions, stew some slices with the other ingredients.

TO CURRY FOWL.

Fry out two or three slices of salt pork; cut the chicken in pieces, and lay it in the stew-pan with one sliced onion; when the fowl is tender, take it out, and put in thickening into the liquor, one spoonful of flour, and one spoonful of curry-powder, well stirred up in water. Then lay the chicken in again, and let it boil up a few minutes. A half a pint of liquor is enough for one chicken. About half an hour's stewing is necessary. The juice of half a lemon improves it; and some like a spoonful of tomatoes catsup.

CHICKEN BROTH.

Cut a chicken in quarters; put it into three or four quarts of water; put in a cup of rice while the water is cold; season it with pepper and salt; some use nutmeg. Let it stew gently, until the chicken falls apart. A little parsley, shred fine, is an improvement. Some slice up a small onion and stew with it. A few pieces of cracker may be thrown in if you like.

A common sized goose should roast full three quarters of an hour. The oil that drips from it should be nearly all turned off; it makes the gravy too greasy; and it is nice for shortening. It should first be turned into cold water; when hardened, it should be taken off and scalded in a skillet. This process leaves it as sweet as lard.

Ducks do not need to be roasted more than fifteen or twenty minutes. Butter melted in boiling flour and water is proper sauce for boiled lamb, mutton, veal, turkeys, geese, chickens, and fish. Some people cut up parsley fine, and throw in. Some people like capers put in. Others heat oysters through on the gridiron, and take them out of the shells, and throw them into the butter.

A good sized turkey should be roasted two hours and a half, or three hours; very slowly at first. If you wish to make plain stuffing, pound a cracker, or crumble some bread very fine, chop some raw salt pork very fine, sift some sage, (and summer-savory, or sweet-marjoram, if you have them in the house, and fancy them,) and mould them all together, seasoned with a little pepper. An egg worked in makes the stuffing cut better; but it is not worth while when eggs are dear. About the same length of time is required for boiling and roasting.

Pigeons may be either roasted, potted or stewed. Potting is the best, and the least trouble. After they are thoroughly picked and cleaned, put a small slice of salt pork, and a little ball of stuffing, into the body of every pigeon. The stuffing should be made of one egg to one cracker, an equal quantity of suet, or butter, seasoned with sweet-marjoram, or sage, if marjoram cannot be procured. Flour the pigeons well, lay them close together in the bottom of the pot, just cover them with water, throw in a bit of butter, and let them stew an hour and a quarter if young; an hour and three quarters if old. Some people turn off the liquor just before they are done, and brown the pigeons on the bottom of the pot; but this is very troublesome, as they are apt to break to pieces.

Stewed pigeons are cooked in nearly the same way, with the omission of the stuffing. Being dry meat, they require a good deal of butter.

Pigeons should be stuffed and roasted about fifteen minutes before a smart fire. Those who like birds just warmed through, would perhaps think less time necessary. It makes them nicer to butter them well just before you take them off the spit, and sprinkle them with nicely pounded bread, or cracker. All poultry should be basted and floured a few minutes before it is taken up.

The age of pigeons can be judged by the color of the legs. When young, they are of a pale delicate brown; as they grow older, the color is deeper and redder.

A nice way of serving up cold chicken, or pieces of cold fresh meat, is to make them into a meat pie. The gizzards, livers, and necks of poultry, parboiled, are good for the same purpose. If you wish to bake your meat pie, line a deep earthen or tin pan with paste made of flour, cold water, and lard; use but little lard, for the fat of the meat will shorten the crust. Lay in your bits of meat, or chicken, with two or three slices of salt pork; place a few thin slices of your paste here and there; drop in an egg or two, if you have plenty. Fill the pan with flour and water, seasoned with a little pepper and salt. If the meat be very lean, put in a piece of butter, or such sweet gravies as you may happen to have. Cover the top with crust, and put it in the oven, or bake-kettle, to cook half an hour, or an hour, according to the size of the pie. Some people think this the nicest way of cooking fresh chickens. When thus cooked, they should be parboiled before they are put into the pan, and the water they are boiled in should be added. A chicken pie needs to be cooked an hour and a half, if parboiled ; two hours, if not.

If you wish to make a pot pie instead of a baked pie, you have only to line the bottom of a porridge pot with paste, lay in your meat, season and moisten it in the same way, cover it with paste, and keep it slowly stewing about the same time that the other takes. In both cases, it is well to lift the upper crust, a little while before you take up the pie, and see whether the moisture has dried away ; if so, pour in flour and water well mixed, and let it boil up.

Potatoes should be boiled in a separate vessel.

If you have fear that poultry may become musty before you want to cook it, skin an onion, and put in it ; a little pepper sprinkled in is good ; it should be kept hung up in a dry, cool place.

If poultry is injured before you are aware of it, wash it very thoroughly in pearlash and water, and sprinkle pepper inside when you cook it. Some people hang up poultry with a muslin bag of charcoal inside. It is a good plan to singe injured poultry over lighted charcoal, and to hold a piece of lighted charcoal inside, a few minutes.

Many people parboil the liver and gizzard, and cut it up very fine, to be put into the gravy, while the fowls are cooking ; in this case, the water they are boiled in should be used to make the gravy.

FISH.

Cod has white stripes, and a haddock black stripes ; they may be known apart by this. Haddock is the best for frying ; and cod is the best for boiling, or for a chowder. A thin tail is a sign of a poor fish ; always choose a thick fish.

When you are buying mackerel, pinch the belly to ascertain whether it is good. If it gives under your finger,
like a bladder half filled with wind, the fish is poor; if it
feels hard like butter, the fish is good. It is cheaper to
buy one large mackerel for ninepence, than two for four
pence half-penny each.

Fish should not be put in to fry until the fat is boiling
hot; it is very necessary to observe this. It should be
dipped in Indian meal before it is put in; and the skinny
side uppermost, when first put in, to prevent its breaking.
It relishes better to be fried after salt pork, than to be fried
in lard alone. People are mistaken, who think fresh fish
should be put into cold water as soon as it is brought into
the house; soaking it in water is injurious. If you want
to keep it sweet, clean it, wash it, wipe it dry with a clean
towel, sprinkle salt inside and out, put it in a covered dish,
and keep it on the *cellar* floor until you want to cook it.
If you live remote from the seaport, and cannot get fish
while hard and fresh, wet it with an egg beaten, before you
meal it, to prevent its breaking.

Fish gravy is very much improved by taking out some
of the fat, after the fish is fried, and putting in a little butter. The fat thus taken out will do to fry fish again; but
it will not do for any kind of shortening. Shake in a little
flour into the hot fat, and pour in a little boiling water;
stir it up well, as it boils, a minute or so. Some people
put in vinegar; but this is easily added by those who
like it.

A common sized cod-fish should be put in when the
water is boiling hot, and boil about twenty minutes. Haddock is not as good for boiling as cod; it takes about the
same time to boil.

A piece of halibut which weighs four pounds is a large
dinner for a family of six or seven. It should boil forty
minutes. No fish put in till the water boils. Melted but
ter for sauce.

Clams should boil about fifteen minutes in their own
water; no other need be added, except a spoonful to keep
the bottom shells from burning. It is easy to tell when

they are done, by the shells starting wide open. After
they are done, they should be taken from the shells, washed thoroughly in their own water, and put in a stewing
pan. The water should then be strained through a cloth,
so as to get out all the grit; the clams should be simmered
in it ten or fifteen minutes; a little thickening of flour and
water added; half a dozen slices of toasted bread or cracker; and pepper, vinegar and butter to your taste. Salt
is not needed.

Four pounds of fish are enough to make a chowder for
four or five people; half a dozen slices of salt pork in the
bottom of the pot; hang it high, so that the pork may not
burn; take it out when done very brown; put in a layer of fish, cut in lengthwise slices, then a layer formed
of crackers, small or sliced onions, and potatoes sliced as
thin as a four-pence, mixed with pieces of pork you have
fried; then a layer of fish again, and so on. Six crackers are enough. Strew a little salt and pepper over each
layer; over the whole pour a bowl-full of flour and water,
enough to come up even with the surface of what you have
in the pot. A sliced lemon adds to the flavor. A cup
of tomato catsup is very excellent. Some people put
in a cup of beer. A few clams are a pleasant addition.
It should be covered so as not to let a particle of steam
escape, if possible. Do not open it, except when nearly
done, to taste if it be well seasoned.

Salt fish should be put in a deep plate, with just water
enough to cover it, the night before you intend to cook it.
It should not be boiled an instant; boiling renders it hard.
It should lie in scalding hot water two or three hours.
The less water is used, and the more fish is cooked at
once, the better. Water thickened with flour and water
while boiling, with sweet butter put in to melt, is the common sauce. It is more economical to cut salt pork into
small bits, and try it till the pork is brown and crispy. It
should not be done too fast, lest the sweetness be scorched out.

Salted shad and mackerel should be put into a deep
plate and covered with boiling water for about ten minutes

after it is thoroughly broiled, before it is buttered. This makes it tender, takes off the coat of salt, and prevents the strong oily taste, so apt to be unpleasant in preserved fish. The same rule applies to smoked salmon.

Salt fish mashed with potatoes, with good butter or pork scraps to moisten it, is nicer the second day than it was the first. The fish should be minced very fine, while it is warm. After it has got cold and dry, it is difficult to do it nicely. Salt fish needs plenty of vegetables, such as onions, beets, carrots, &c.

There is no way of preparing salt fish for breakfast, so nice as to roll it up in little balls, after it is mixed with mashed potatoes; dip it into an egg, and fry it brown.

A female lobster is not considered so good as a male. In the female, the sides of the head, or what look like cheeks, are much larger, and jut out more than those of the male. The end of a lobster is surrounded with what children call 'purses,' edged with a little fringe. If you put your hand under these to raise it, and find it springs back hard and firm, it is a sign the lobster is fresh; if they move flabbily, it is not a good omen.

Fried salt pork and apples is a favorite dish in the country; but it is seldom seen in the city. After the pork is fried, some of the fat should be taken out, lest the apples should be oily. Acid apples should be chosen, because they cook more easily; they should be cut in slices, across the whole apple, about twice or three times as thick as a new dollar. Fried till tender, and brown on both sides—laid around the pork. If you have cold potatoes, slice them and brown them in the same way.

PUDDINGS.

BAKED INDIAN PUDDING.

INDIAN pudding is good baked. Scald a quart of milk (skimmed milk will do,) and stir in seven table spoonfuls of sifted Indian meal, a tea-spoonful of salt, a tea-cupful of molasses, and a great spoonful of ginger, or sifted cinnamon. Baked three or four hours. If you want whey, you must be sure and pour in a little cold milk, after it is all mixed.

BOILED INDIAN PUDDING.

Indian pudding should be boiled four or five hours. Sifted Indian meal and warm milk should be stirred together pretty stiff. A little salt, and two or three great spoonfuls of molasses, added; a spoonful of ginger, if you like that spice. Boil it in a tight covered pan, or a very thick cloth; if the water gets in, it will ruin it. Leave plenty of room; for Indian swells very much. The milk with which you mix it should be merely warm ; if it be scalding, the pudding will break to pieces. Some people chop sweet suet fine, and warm in the milk; others warm thin slices of sweet apple to be stirred into the pudding. Water will answer instead of milk.

FLOUR OR BATTER PUDDING.

Common flour pudding, or batter pudding, is easily made. Those who live in the country can beat up five or six eggs with a quart of milk, and a little salt, with flour enough to make it just thick enough to pour without difficulty. Those who live in the city, and are obliged to buy eggs, can do with three eggs to a quart, and more flour in proportion. Boil about three quarters of an hour.

BREAD PUDDING.

A nice pudding may be made of bits of bread. They should be crumbled and soaked in milk over night. In the morning, beat up three eggs with it, add a little salt, tie it up in a bag, or in a pan that will exclude every drop of water, and boil it little more than an hour. No puddings should be put into the pot, till the water boils. Bread prepared in the same way makes good plum-puddings. Milk enough to make it quite soft; four eggs; a little cinnamon; a spoonful of rose-water, or lemon-brandy, if you have it; a tea-cupful of molasses, or sugar to your taste, if you prefer it; a few dry, clean raisins, sprinkled in, and stirred up thoroughly, is all that is necessary. It should bake or boil two hours.

RENNET PUDDING.

If your husband brings home company when you are unprepared, rennet pudding may be made at five minutes' notice; provided you keep a piece of calf's rennet ready prepared soaking in a bottle of wine. One glass of this wine to a quart of milk will make a sort of cold custard. Sweetened with white sugar, and spiced with nutmeg, it is very good. It should be eaten immediately; in a few hours, it begins to curdle.

CUSTARD PUDDINGS.

Custard puddings sufficiently good for common use can be made with five eggs to a quart of milk, sweetened with brown sugar, and spiced with cinnamon, or nutmeg, and very little salt. It is well to boil your milk, and set it away till it gets cold. Boiling milk enriches it so much, that boiled skim-milk is about as good as new milk. A little cinnamon, or lemon peel, or peach leaves, if you do not dislike the taste, boiled in the milk, and afterwards strained from it, give a pleasant flavor. Bake fifteen or twenty minutes.

RICE PUDDINGS.

If you want a common rice pudding to retain its flavor, do not soak it, or put it in to boil when the water is cold. Wash it, tie it in a bag, leave plenty of room for it to swell, throw it in when the water boils, and let it boil about an hour and a half. The same sauce answers for all these kinds of puddings. If you have rice left cold, break it up in a little warm milk, pour custard over it, and bake it as long as you should custard. It makes very good puddings and pies.

BIRD'S NEST PUDDING.

If you wish to make what is called 'bird's nest puddings,' prepare your custard,—take eight or ten pleasant apples, pare them, and dig out the core, but leave them whole, set them in a pudding dish, pour your custard over them, and bake them about thirty minutes.

APPLE PUDDING.

A plain, unexpensive apple pudding may be made by rolling out a bit of common pie-crust, and filling it full of quartered apples; tied up in a bag, and boiled an hour and a half; if the apples are sweet, it will take two hours; for acid things cook easily. Some people like little dumplings, made by rolling up one apple, pared and cored, in a piece of crust, and tying them up in spots all over the bag. These do not need to be boiled more than an hour: three quarters is enough, if the apples are tender.

Take sweet, or pleasant flavored apples, pare them, and bore out the core, without cutting the apple in two Fill up the holes with washed rice, boil them in a bag, tied very tight, an hour, or hour and a half. Each apple should be tied up separately, in different corners of the pudding bag

CHERRY PUDDING.

For cherry dumpling, make a paste about as rich as you make short-cake; roll it out, and put in a pint and a half,

or a quart of cherries, according to the size of your family.
Double the crust over the fruit, tie it up tight in a bag,
and boil one hour and a half.

CRANBERRY PUDDING.

A pint of cranberries stirred into a quart of batter, made
like a batter pudding, but very little stiffer, is very nice,
eaten with sweet sauce.

WHORTLEBERRY PUDDING.

Whortleberries are good both in flour and Indian puddings. A pint of milk, with a little salt and a little molasses, stirred quite stiff with Indian meal, and a quart of berries stirred in gradually with a spoon, makes a good-sized
pudding. Leave room for it to swell; and let it boil three
hours.

When you put them into flour, make your pudding just
like batter puddings; but considerably thicker, or the berries will sink. Two hours is plenty long enough to boil.
No pudding should be put in till the water boils. Leave
room to swell.

PLUM PUDDING.

If you wish to make a really nice, soft, custard-like plum
pudding, pound six crackers, or dried crusts of light
bread, fine, and soak them over night in milk enough to
cover them; put them in about three pints of milk, beat up
six eggs, put in a little lemon-brandy, a whole nutmeg,
and about three quarters of a pound of raisins which have
been rubbed in flour. Bake it two hours, or perhaps a
little short of that. It is easy to judge from the appearance
whether it is done.

The surest way of making a light, rich plum pudding, is
to spread slices of sweet light bread plentifully with butter; on each side of the slices spread abundantly raisins, or
currants, nicely prepared; when they are all heaped up in
a dish, cover them with milk, eggs, sugar and spice, well

beat up, and prepared just as you do for custards. Let it
bake about an hour.

One sauce answers for common use for all sorts of
puddings. Flour-and-water stirred into boiling water,
sweetened to your taste with either molasses or sugar, according to your ideas of economy ; a great spoonful of rose-
water, if you have it ; butter half as big as a hen's egg. If
you want to make it very nice, put in a glass of wine, and
grate nutmeg on the top.

When you wish better sauce than common, take a quarter of a pound of butter and the same of sugar, mould them
well together with your hand, add a little wine, if you
choose. Make it into a lump, set it away to cool, and
grate nutmeg over it.

HASTY PUDDING.

Boil water, a quart, three pints, or two quarts, according
to the size of your family ; sift your meal, stir five or six
spoonfuls of it thoroughly into a bowl of water ; when the
water in the kettle boils, pour into it the contents of the bowl ;
stir it well, and let it boil up thick ; put in salt to suit your
own taste, then stand over the kettle, and sprinkle in meal,
handful after handful, stirring it very thoroughly all the
time, and letting it boil between whiles. When it is so
thick that you stir it with great difficulty, it is about right.
It takes about half an hour's cooking. Eat it with milk or
molasses. Either Indian meal or rye meal may be used.
If the system is in a restricted state, nothing can be better than *rye* hasty pudding and *West India* molasses.
This diet would save many a one the horrors of dyspepsia.

CHEAP CUSTARDS.

ONE quart of milk, boiled ; when boiling, add three table spoonfuls of ground rice, or rice that is boiled, mixed

smooth and fine in cold milk, and one egg beaten ; give it one boil up, and sweeten to your taste ; peach leaves, or any spice you please, boiled in the milk.

COMMON PIES.

MINCE PIES.

Boil a tender, nice piece of beef—any piece that is clear from sinews and gristle ; boil it till it is perfectly tender. When it is cold, chop it very fine, and be very careful to get out every particle of bone and gristle. The suet is sweeter and better to boil half an hour or more in the liquor the beef has been boiled in ; but few people do this. Pare, core, and chop the apples fine. If you use raisins, stone them. If you use currants, wash and dry them at the fire. Two pounds of beef, after it is chopped ; three quarters of a pound of suet ; one pound and a quarter of sugar ; three pounds of apples ; two pounds of currants, or raisins. Put in a gill of brandy ; lemon-brandy is better, if you have any prepared. Make it quite moist with new cider. I should not think a quart would be too much ; the more moist the better, if it does not spill out into the oven. A very little pepper. If you use corn meat, or tongue, for pies, it should be well soaked, and boiled very tender. If you use fresh beef, salt is necessary in the seasoning. One ounce of cinnamon, one ounce of cloves. Two nutmegs add to the pleasantness of the flavor ; and a bit of sweet butter put upon the top of each pie, makes them rich ; but these are not necessary. Baked three quarters of an hour. If your apples are rather sweet, grate in a whole lemon.

PUMPKIN AND SQUASH PIE.

For common family pumpkin pies, three eggs do very well to a quart of milk. Stew your pumpkin, and strain it through a sieve, or colander. Take out the seeds, and pare the pumpkin, or squash, before you stew it; but do not scrape the inside; the part nearest the seed is the sweetest part of the squash. Stir in the stewed pumpkin, till it is as thick as you can stir it round rapidly and easily. If you want to make your pie richer, make it thinner, and add another egg. One egg to a quart of milk makes very decent pies. Sweeten it to your taste, with molasses or sugar; some pumpkins require more sweetening than others. Two tea-spoonfuls of salt; two great spoonfuls of sifted cinnamon; one great spoonful of ginger. Ginger will answer very well alone for spice, if you use enough of it. The outside of a lemon grated in is nice. The more eggs, the better the pie; some put an egg to a gill of milk. They should bake from forty to fifty minutes, and even ten minutes longer, if very deep.

CARROT PIE.

Carrot pies are made like squash pies. The carrots should be boiled very tender, skinned and sifted. Both carrot pies and squash pies should be baked without an upper crust, in deep plates. To be baked an hour, in quite a warm oven.

CHERRY PIE.

Cherry pies should be baked in a deep plate. Take the cherries from the stalks, lay them in a plate, and sprinkle a little sugar, and cinnamon, according to the sweetness of the cherries. Baked with a top and bottom crust, three quarters of an hour.

WHORTLEBERRY PIE.

Whortleberries make a very good common pie, where there is a large family of children. Sprinkle a little sugar and sifted cloves into each pie. Baked in the same way, and as long, as cherry pies.

APPLE PIE.

When you make apple pies, stew your apples very little indeed; just strike them through, to make them tender.

Some people do not stew them at all, but cut them up in very thin slices, and lay them in the crust. Pies made in this way may retain more of the spirit of the apple ; but I do not think the seasoning mixes in as well. Put in sugar to your taste ; it is impossible to make a precise rule, because apples vary so much in acidity. A very little salt, and a small piece of butter in each pie, makes them richer. Cloves and cinnamon are both suitable spice. Lemon-brandy and rose-water are both excellent. A wine-glass full of each is sufficient for three or four pies. If your apples lack spirit, grate in a whole lemon.

CUSTARD PIE.

It is a general rule to put eight eggs to a quart of milk, in making custard pies ; but six eggs are a plenty for any common use. The milk should be boiled and cooled before it is used ; and bits of stick-cinnamon and bits of lemon-peel boiled in it. Sweeten to your taste with clean sugar ; a very little sprinkling of salt makes them taste better. Grate in a nutmeg. Bake in a deep plate. About 20 minutes are usually enough. If you are doubtful whether they are done, dip in the handle of a silver spoon, or the blade of a small knife ; if it come out clean, the pie is done. Do not pour them into your plates till the minute you put them into the oven ; it makes the crust wet and heavy. To be baked with an under crust only. Some people bake the under crust a little before the custard is poured in ; this is to keep it from being clammy.

CRANBERRY PIE.

Cranberry pies need very little spice. A little nutmeg, or cinnamon, improves them. They need a great deal of sweetening. It is well to stew the sweetening with them ; at least a part of it. It is easy to add, if you find them too sour for your taste. When cranberries are strained, and added to about their own weight in sugar, they make very delicious tarts. No upper crust.

RHUBARB STALKS, OR PERSIAN APPLE.

Rhubarb stalks, or the Persian apple, is the earliest in gredient for pies, which the spring offers. The skin should be carefully stripped, and the stalks cut into small bits, and stewed very tender. These are dear pies, for they take an enormous quantity of sugar. Seasoned like apple pies Gooseberries, currants, &c., are stewed, sweetened and seasoned like apple pies, in proportions suited to the sweetness of the fruit; there is no way to judge but by your own taste. Always remember it is more easy to add seasoning than to diminish it.

PIE CRUST.

To make pie crust for common use, a quarter of a pound of butter is enough for a half a pound of flour. Take out about a quarter part of the flour you intend to use, and lay it aside. Into the remainder of the flour rub butter thoroughly with your hands, until it is so short that a handful of it, clasped tight, will remain in a ball, without any tendency to fall in pieces. Then wet it with cold water, roll it out on a board, rub over the surface with flour, stick little lumps of butter all over it, sprinkle some flour over the butter, and roll the dough all up; flour the paste, and flour the rolling-pin; roll it lightly and quickly; flour it again; stick in bits of butter; do it up; flour the rolling-pin, and roll it quickly and lightly; and so on, till you have used up your butter. Always roll from you. Pie crust should be made as cold as possible, and set in a cool place; but be careful it does not freeze. Do not use more flour than you can help in sprinkling and rolling. The paste should not be rolled out more than three times; if rolled too much, it will not be flaky.

COMMON CAKES.

In all cakes where butter or eggs are used, the butter should be very faithfully rubbed into the flour, and the eggs beat to a foam, before the ingredients are mixed.

GINGERBREAD.

A very good way to make molasses gingerbread is to rub four pounds and a half of flour with half a pound of lard and half a pound of butter; a pint of molasses, a gill of milk, tea-cup of ginger, a tea-spoonful of dissolved pearlash stirred together. All mixed, baked in shallow pans twenty or thirty m nutes.

Hard gingerbread is good to have in the family, it keeps so well. One pound of flour, half a pound of butter and sugar, rubbed into it; half a pound of sugar; great spoonful of ginger, or more, according to the strength of the ginger; a spoonful of rose-water, and a handful of caraway seed. Well beat up. Kneaded stiff enough to roll out and bake on flat pans. Bake twenty or thirty minutes.

A cake of common gingerbread can be stirred up very quick in the following way. Rub in a bit of shortening as big as an egg into a pint of flour; if you use lard, add a little salt; two or three great spoonfuls of ginger; one cup of molasses, one cup and a half of cider, and a great spoonful of dissolved pearlash, put together and poured into the shortened flour while it is foaming; to be put in the oven in a minute. It ought to be just thick enough to pour into the pans with difficulty; if these proportions make it too thin, use less liquid the next time you try. Bake about twenty minutes.

If by carelessness you let a piece of short-cake dough grow sour, put in a little pearlash and water, warm a little butter, according to the size of the dough, knead in a cup or two of sugar, (two cups, unless it is a very small bit,) two or three spoonfuls of ginger, and a little rose-water

Knead it up thoroughly, roll it out on a flat pan, and bake it twenty minutes. Every thing mixed with pearlash should be put in the oven immediately.

CUP CAKE.

Cup cake is about as good as pound cake, and is cheaper. One cup of butter, two cups of sugar, three cups of flour, and four eggs, well beat together, and baked in pans or cups. Bake twenty minutes, and no more.

TEA CAKE.

There is a kind of tea cake still cheaper. Three cups of sugar, three eggs, one cup of butter, one cup of milk, a spoonful of dissolved pearlash, and four cups of flour, well beat up. If it is so stiff it will not stir easily, add a little more milk.

CIDER CAKE.

Cider cake is very good, to be baked in small loaves. One pound and a half of flour, half a pound of sugar, quarter of a pound of butter, half a pint of cider, one teaspoonful of pearlash; spice to your taste. Bake till it turns easily in the pans. I should think about half an hour.

ELECTION CAKE.

Old-fashioned election cake is made of four pounds of flour; three quarters of a pound of butter; four eggs; one pound of sugar; one pound of currants, or raisins if you choose; half a pint of good yeast; wet it with milk as soft as it can be and be moulded on a board. Set to rise over night in winter; in warm weather, three hours is usually enough for it to rise. A loaf, the size of common flour bread, should bake three quarters of an hour.

SPONGE CAKE.

The nicest way to make sponge cake, or diet-bread, is the weight of six eggs in sugar, the weight of four eggs in flour, a little rose-water. The whites and yolks should be beaten thoroughly and separately. The eggs and sugar should be well beaten together; but after the flour is sprinkled, it should not be stirred a moment longer than is necessary to mix it well; it should be poured into the pan, and got into the oven with all possible expedition. Twenty minutes is about long enough to bake. Not to be put in till some other articles have taken off the first few minutes of furious heat.

WEDDING CAKE.

Good common wedding cake may be made thus : Four pounds of flour, three pounds of butter, three pounds of sugar, four pounds of currants, two pounds of raisins, twenty-four eggs, half a pint of brandy, or lemon-brandy, one ounce of mace, and three nutmegs. A little molasses makes it dark colored, which is desirable. Half a pound of citron improves it; but it is not necessary. To be baked two hours and a half, or three hours. After the oven is cleared, it is well to shut the door for eight or ten minutes, to let the violence of the heat subside, before cake or bread is put in.

To make icing for your wedding cake, beat the whites of eggs to an entire froth, and to each egg add five teaspoonfuls of sifted loaf sugar, gradually; beat it a great while. Put it on when your cake is hot, or cold, as is most convenient. It will dry in a warm room, a short distance from a gentle fire, or in a warm oven.

LOAF CAKE.

Very good loaf cake is made with two pounds of flour, half a pound of sugar, quarter of a pound of butter, two eggs, a gill of sweet emptings, half an ounce of cinnamon, or cloves, a large spoonful of lemon-brandy, or rose-water; if it is not about as thin as good white bread dough, add a little milk. A common sized loaf is made by these proportions. Bake about three quarters of an hour.

A handy way to make loaf cake is, to take about as much of your white bread dough, or sponge, as you think your pan will hold, and put it into a pan in which you have already beat up three or four eggs, six ounces of butter warmed, and half a pound of sugar, a spoonful of rose-water, little sifted cinnamon, or cloves. The materials should be well mixed and beat before the dough is put in ; and then it should be all kneaded well together, about as stiff as white bread. Put in half a pound of currants, or raisins, with the butter, if you choose. It should stand in the pan two or three hours to rise ; and be baked about three quarters of an hour, if the pan is a common sized bread-pan.

If you have loaf cake slightly injured by time, or by being kept in the cellar, cut off all appearance of mould from the outside, wipe it with a clean cloth, and wet it well with strong brandy and water sweetened with sugar ; then put it in your oven, and let the heat strike through it, for fifteen or twenty minutes. Unless very bad, this will restore the sweetness.

CARAWAY CAKES.

Take one pound of flour, three quarters of a pound of sugar, half a pound of butter, a glass of rose-water, four eggs, and half a tea-cup of caraway seed,—the materials well rubbed together and beat up. Drop them from a spoon on tin sheets, and bake them brown in rather a slow oven. Twenty minutes, or half an hour, is enough to bake them.

DOUGH-NUTS.

For dough-nuts, take one pint of flour, half a pint of sugar, three eggs, a piece of butter as big as an egg, and a tea-spoonful of dissolved pearlash. When you have no eggs, a gill of lively emptings will do ; but in that case, they must be made over night. Cinnamon, rose-water, or lemon-brandy, if you have it. If you use part lard instead of butter, add a little salt. Not put in till the fat is very hot. The more fat they are fried in, the less they will soak fat.

PANCAKES.

Pancakes should be made of half a pint of milk, three great spoonfuls of sugar, one or two eggs, a tea-spoonful of dissolved pearlash, spiced with cinnamon, or cloves, a little salt, rose-water, or lemon-brandy, just as you happen to have it. Flour should be stirred in till the spoon moves round with difficulty. If they are thin, they are apt to soak fat. Have the fat in your skillet boiling hot, and drop them in with a spoon. Let them cook till thoroughly brown. The fat which is left is good to shorten other cakes. The more fat they are cooked in, the less they soak.

If you have no eggs, or wish to save them, use the above ingredients, and supply the place of eggs by two or three spoonfuls of lively emptings; but in this case they must be made five or six hours before they are cooked,— and in winter they should stand all night. A spoonful or more of N. E. rum makes pancakes light. Flip makes very nice pancakes. In this case, nothing is done but to sweeten your mug of beer with molasses; put in one glass of N. E. rum; heat it till it foams, by putting in a hot poker; and stir it up with flour as thick as other pancakes.

FRITTERS.

Flat-jacks, or fritters, do not differ from pancakes, only in being mixed softer. The same ingredients are used in about the same quantities; only most people prefer to have no sweetening put in them, because they generally have butter, sugar, and nutmeg, put on them, after they are done. Excepting for company, the nutmeg can be well dispensed with. They are not to be boiled in fat, like pancakes; the spider or griddle should be well greased, and the cakes poured on as large as you want them, when it is quite hot; when it gets brown on one side, to be turned over upon the other. Fritters are better to be baked quite thin. Either flour, Indian, or rye, is good.

Sour beer, with a spoonful of pearlash, is good both for pancakes and fritters.

If you have any cold rice left, it is nice to break it up fine in warm milk ; put in a little salt ; after you have put milk enough for the cakes you wish to make, (a half pint, or more,) stir in flour till it is thick enough to pour for fritters. It does very well without an egg ; but better with one. To be fried like other flat-jacks. Sugar and nutmeg are to be put on when they are buttered, if you like.

SHORT CAKE.

If you have sour milk, or butter-milk, it is well to make it into short cakes for tea. Rub in a very small bit of shortening, or three table-spoonfuls of cream, with the flour ; put in a tea-spoonful of strong dissolved pearlash, into your sour milk, and mix your cake pretty stiff, to bake in the spider, on a few embers.

When people have to buy butter and lard, short cakes are not economical food. A half pint of flour will make a cake large enough to cover a common plate. Rub in thoroughly a bit of shortening as big as a hen's egg ; put in a tea-spoonful of dissolved pearlash ; wet it with cold water ; knead it stiff enough to roll well, to bake on a plate, or in a spider. It should bake as quick as it can, and not burn. The first side should stand longer to the fire than the last.

INDIAN CAKE.

Indian cake, or bannock, is sweet and cheap food. One quart of sifted meal, two great spoonfuls of molasses, two tea-spoonfuls of salt, a bit of shortening half as big as a hen's egg, stirred together ; make it pretty moist with scalding water, put it into a well greased pan, smooth over the surface with a spoon, and bake it brown on both sides, before a quick fire. A little stewed pumpkin, scalded with the meal, improves the cake. Bannock split and dipped in butter makes very nice toast.

A richer Indian cake may be made by stirring one egg to a half pint of milk, sweetened with two great spoonfuls of molasses ; a little ginger, or cinnamon ; Indian stirred in till it is just about thick enough to pour. Spider or bake-kettle well greased; cake poured in, covered up, baked half an hour, or three quarters, according to the thickness of the cake. If you have sour milk, or butter-milk, it is very nice for this kind of cake ; the acidity corrected by a tea-spoonful of dissolved pearlash. It is a rule never to use pearlash for Indian, unless to correct the sourness of milk; it injures the flavor of the meal.

Nice suet improves all kinds of Indian cakes very much.

—

Two cups of Indian meal, one table-spoonful molasses, two cups milk, a little salt, a handful flour, a little saleratus, mixed up thin, and poured into a buttered bake-kettle, hung over the fire uncovered, until you can bear your finger upon it, and then set down before the fire. Bake half an hour.

BREAD, YEAST, &c.

It is more difficult to give rules for making bread than for anything else ; it depends so much on judgment and experience. In summer, bread should be mixed with cold water ; during a chilly, damp spell, the water should be slightly warm ; in severe cold weather, it should be mixed quite warm, and set in a warm place during the night. If your yeast is new and lively, a small quantity will make the bread rise ; if it be old and heavy, it will take more. In these things I believe wisdom must be gained by a few mistakes.

Six quarts of meal will make two good sized loaves of *Brown Bread*. Some like to have it half Indian meal and half rye meal ; others prefer it one third Indian, and

two thirds rye. Many mix their brown bread over night;
but there is no need of it; and it is more likely to sour,
particularly in summer. If you do mix it the night
before you bake it, you must not put in more than half the
yeast I am about to mention, unless the weather is intense-
ly cold. The meal should be sifted separately. Put the
Indian in your bread-pan, sprinkle a little salt among it, and
wet it thoroughly with scalding water. Stir it up while
you are scalding it. Be sure and have hot water enough;
for Indian absorbs a great deal of water. When it is cool,
pour in your rye; add two gills of lively yeast, and mix it
with water as stiff as you can knead it. Let it stand an hour
and a half, in a cool place in summer, on the hearth in
winter. It should be put into a very hot oven, and baked
three or four hours. It is all the better for remaining in
the oven over night.

Flour Bread should have a sponge set the night before.
The sponge should be soft enough to pour; mixed with
water, warm or cold, according to the temperature of the
weather. One gill of lively yeast is enough to put into
sponge for two loaves. I should judge about three pints
of sponge would be right for two loaves. The warmth of
the place in which the sponge is set, should be determined by the coldness of the weather. If your sponge looks
frothy in the morning, it is a sign your bread will be good;
if it does not rise, stir in a little more emptings; if it rises
too much, taste of it, to see if it has any acid taste; if so,
put in a tea-spoonful of pearlash when you mould in your
flour; be sure the pearlash is well dissolved in water; if
there are little lumps, your bread will be full of bitter spots.
About an hour before your oven is ready, stir in flour into
your sponge till it is stiff enough to lay on a well floured
board or table. Knead it up pretty stiff, and put it into
well greased pans, and let it stand in a cool or warm place,
according to the weather. If the oven is ready, put them
in fifteen or twenty minutes after the dough begins to
rise up and crack; if the oven is not ready, move the pans
to a cooler spot, to prevent the dough from becoming sour
by too much rising. Common sized loaves will bake in

three quarters of an hour. If they slip easily in the pans, it is a sign they are done. Some people do not set a soft sponge for flour bread; they knead it up all ready to put in the pans the night before, and leave it to rise. White bread and pies should not be set in the oven until the brown bread and beans have been in half an hour. If the oven be too hot, it will bind the crust so suddenly that the bread cannot rise; if it be too cold, the bread will fall. Flour bread should not be too stiff.

Some people like one third Indian in their flour. Others like one third rye; and some think the nicest of all bread is one third Indian, one third rye, and one third flour, made according to the directions for flour bread. When Indian is used, it should be salted, and scalded, before the other meal is put in. A mixture of other grains is economical when flour is high.

Dyspepsia Bread.—The American Farmer publishes the following receipt for making bread, which has proved highly salutary to persons afflicted with that complaint, viz:—Three quarts unbolted wheat meal; one quart soft water, warm, but not hot; one gill of fresh yeast; one gill of molasses, or not, as may suit the taste; one tea-spoonful of saleratus.

This will make two loaves, and should remain in the oven at least one hour; and when taken out, placed where they will cool gradually. Dyspepsia crackers can be made with unbolted flour, water and saleratus.

To make Rice Bread.—Boil a pint of rice soft; add a pint of leaven; then, three quarts of the flour; put it to rise in a tin or earthen vessel until it has risen sufficiently; divide it into three parts; then bake it as other bread, and you will have three large loaves.

Heating ovens must be regulated by experience and observation. There is a difference in wood in giving out heat; there is a great difference in the construction of ovens; and when an oven is extremely cold, either on account of the weather, or want of use, it must be heated more. Economical people heat ovens with pine wood, fagots, brush, and such light stuff. If you have none but hard wood, you must remember that it makes very hot coals, and therefore less of it will answer. A smart fire for an hour and a half is a general rule for common sized family ovens, provided brown bread and beans are to be baked. An hour is long enough to heat an oven for flour bread. Pies bear about as much heat as flour bread : pumpkin pies will bear more. If you are afraid your oven is too hot, throw in a little flour, and shut it up for a minute. If it scorches black immediately, the heat is too furious ; if it merely browns, it is right. Some people wet an old broom two or three times, and turn it round near the top of the oven till it dries; this prevents pies and cake from scorching on the top. When you go into a new house, heat your oven two or three times, to get it seasoned, before you use it. After the wood is burned, rake the coals over the bottom of the oven, and let them lie a few minutes.

Those who make their own bread should make yeast too. When bread is nearly out, always think whether yeast is in readiness; for it takes a day and night to prepare it. One handful of hops, with two or three handsful of malt and rye bran, should be boiled fifteen or twenty minutes, in two quarts of water, then strained, hung on to boil again, and thickened with half a pint of rye and water stirred up quite thick, and a little molasses; boil it a minute or two, and then take it off to cool. When just about lukewarm, put in a cupful of good lively yeast, and set it in a cool place in summer, and warm place in winter. If it is too warm when you put in the old yeast, all the spirit will be killed.

In summer, yeast sours easily; therefore make but little at a time. Bottle it when it gets well a working; it keeps better when the air is corked out. If you find it acid, but still spirited, put a little pearlash to it, as you use it; but by no means put it into your bread unless it foams up bright and lively as soon as the pearlash mixes with it. Never keep yeast in tin ; it destroys its life.

There is another method of making yeast, which is much easier, and I think quite as good. Stir rye and cold water, till you make a stiff thickening. Then pour in boiling water, and stir it all the time, till you make it as thin as the yeast you buy; three or four table spoons heaping full are enough for a quart of water. When it gets about cold, put in half a pint of lively yeast. When it works well, bottle it; but if very lively, do not cork your bottle *very* tight, for fear it will burst. Always think to make new yeast before the old is gone; so that you may have some to work with. Always wash and scald your bottle clean after it has contained sour yeast. Beware of freezing yeast.

Milk yeast is made quicker than any other. A pint of new milk with a tea-spoonful of salt, and a large spoon of flour stirred in, set by the fire to keep lukewarm, will make yeast fit for use in an hour. Twice the quantity of com mon yeast is necessary, and unless used soon is good for nothing. Bread made of this yeast dries sooner. It is convenient in summer, when one wants to make biscuits suddenly.

A species of leaven may be made that will keep any length of time. Three ounces of hops in a pail of water boiled down to a quart; strain it, and stir in a quart of rye meal while boiling hot. Cool it, and add half a pint of good yeast; after it has risen a few hours, thicken it with In dian meal stiff enough to roll out upon a board; then put it in the sun and air a few days to dry. A piece of this cake two inches square, dissolved in warm water, and thickened with a little flour, will make a large loaf of bread.

Potatoes make very good yeast. Mash three large potatoes fine; pour a pint of boiling water over them; when almost cold, stir in two spoonfuls of flour, two of molasses, and a cup of good yeast. This yeast should be used while new.

PRESERVES, &c.

Economical people will seldom use preserves, except for sickness. They are unhealthy, expensive, and useless to those who are well. Barberries preserved in molasses are very good for common use. Boil the molasses, skim it, throw in the barberries, and simmer them till they are soft. If you wish to lay by a few for sickness, preserve them in sugar by the same rule as other preserves. Melt the sugar, skim it, throw in the barberries; when done soft, take them out, and throw in others.

A pound of sugar to a pound of fruit is the rule for all preserves. The sugar should be melted over a fire moderate enough not to scorch it. When melted, it should be skimmed clean, and the fruit dropped in to simmer till it is soft. Plums, and things of which the skin is liable to be broken, do better to be put in little jars, with their weight of sugar, and the jars set in a kettle of boiling water, till the fruit is done. See the water is not so high as to boil into the jars.

When you put preserves in jars, lay a white paper, thoroughly wet with brandy, flat upon the surface of the preserves, and cover them carefully from the air. If they begin to mould, scald them by setting them in the oven till boiling hot. Glass is much better than earthen for preserves; they are not half as apt to ferment.

CURRANT JELLY.

Currant jelly is a useful thing for sickness. If it be necessary to wash your currants, be sure they are thoroughly drained, or your jelly will be thin. Break them up with a pestle, and squeeze them through a cloth. Put a pint of clean sugar to a pint of juice, and boil it slowly, till it becomes ropy. Great care must be taken not to do it too fast; it is spoiled by being scorched. It should be frequently skimmed while simmering. If currants are put

in a jar, and kept in boiling water, and cooked before they
are strained, they are more likely to keep a long time without fermenting.

CURRANT WINE.

Those who have more currants than they have money,
will do well to use no wine but of their own manufacture.
Break and squeeze the currants, put three pounds and a
half of sugar to two quarts of juice and two quarts of water. Put 'n a keg or barrel. Do not close the bung tight
for three or four days, that the air may escape while it is
fermenting. After it is done fermenting, close it up tight.
Where raspberries are plenty, it is a great improvement
to use half raspberry juice, and half currant juice. Brandy is unnecessary when the above-mentioned proportions are observed. It should not be used under a year
or two. Age improves it.

RASPBERRY SHRUB.

Raspberry shrub mixed with water is a pure, delicious
drink for summer ; and in a country where raspberries are
abundant, it is good economy to make it answer instead
of Port and Catalonia wine. Put raspberries in a pan, and
scarcely cover them with strong vinegar. Add a pint of
sugar to a pint of juice ; (of this you can judge by first
trying your pan to see how much it holds ;) scald it, skim
it, and bottle it when cold.

COFFEE.

As substitutes for coffee, some use dry brown bread
crusts, and roast them ; others soak rye grain in rum, and
roast it ; others roast peas in the same way as coffee.
None of these are very good ; and peas so used are considered unhealthy. Where there is a large family of appren-
tices and workmen, and coffee is very dear, it may be
worth while to use the substitutes, or to mix them half and
half with coffee ; but, after all, the best economy is to go
without.

French coffee is so celebrated, that it may be worth while to tell how it is made ; though no prudent house-keeper will make it, unless she has boarders, who are will-ing to pay for expensive cooking.

The coffee should be roasted more than is common with us ; it should not hang drying over the fire, but should be roasted quick ; it should be ground soon after roasting, and used as soon as it is ground. Those who pride them-selves on first-rate coffee, burn it and grind it every morn-ing. The powder should be placed in the coffee-pot in the proportions of an ounce to less than a pint of water. The water should be poured upon the coffee boiling hot. The coffee should be kept at the boiling point; but should not boil. Coffee made in this way must be made in a biggin. It would not be clear in a common coffee-pot.

A bit of fish-skin as big as a ninepence, thrown into cof-fee while it is boiling, tends to make it clear. If you use it just as it comes from the salt-fish, it will be apt to give an unpleasant taste to the coffee : it should be washed clean as a bit of cloth, and hung up till perfectly dry. The white of eggs, and even egg shells are good to settle coffee. Rind of salt pork is excellent.

Some people think coffee is richer and clearer for hav-ing a bit of sweet butter, or a whole egg, dropped in and stirred, just before it is done roasting, and ground up, shell and all, with the coffee. But these things are not economi-cal, except on a farm, where butter and eggs are plenty. A half a gill of cold water, poured in after you take your cof-fee-pot off the fire, will *usually* settle the coffee.

If you have not cream for coffee, it is a very great im-provement to boil your milk, and use it while hot.

CHOCOLATE.

Many people boil chocolate in a coffee-pot ; but I think it is better to boil it in a skillet, or something open. A piece of chocolate about as big as a dollar is the usual quan-tity for a quart of water ; but some put in more, and some less When it boils, pour in as much milk as you like

and let them boil together three or four minutes. It is
much richer with the milk boiled in it. Put the sugar in
either before or after, as you please. Nutmeg improves
it. The chocolate should be scraped fine before it is put
into the water.

TEA.

Young Hyson is supposed to be a more profitable tea
than Hyson ; but though the *quantity* to a pound is greater,
it has not so much *strength.* In point of economy, therefore, there is not much difference between them. Hyson tea
and Souchong mixed together, half and half, is a pleasant
beverage, and is more healthy than green tea alone. Be
sure that water boils before it is poured upon tea. A
tea-spoonful to each person, and one extra thrown in, is a
good rule. Steep ten or fifteen minutes.

PICKLES.

Musk-melons should be picked for mangoes, when they
are green and hard. They should be cut open after they
have been in salt water ten days, the inside scraped out
clean, and filled with mustard-seed, allspice, horseradish,
small onions, &c., and sewed up again. Scalding vinegar
poured upon them.

When walnuts are so ripe that a pin will go into them
easily, they are ready for pickling. They should be soaked twelve days in very strong cold salt and water, which has
been boiled and skimmed. A quantity of vinegar, enough
to cover them well, should be boiled with whole pepper,
mustard-seed, small onions, or garlic, cloves, ginger, and
horseradish ; this should not be poured upon them till it
is cold. They should be pickled a few months before
they are eaten. To be kept close covered ; for the air
softens them. The liquor is an excellent catsup to be
eaten on fish.

Put peppers into strong salt and water, until they become
yellow ; then turn them green by keeping them in warm
salt and water, shifting them every two days. Then drain

them, and pour scalding vinegar over them. A bag of mustard-seed is an improvement. If there is mother in vinegar, scald and strain it.

Cucumbers should be in weak brine three or four days after they are picked; then they should be put in a tin or wooden pail of clean water, and kept slightly warm in the kitchen corner for two or three days. Then take as much vinegar as you think your pickle jar will hold; scald it with pepper, allspice, mustard-seed, flag-root, horseradish, &c., if you happen to have them; half of them will spice the pickles very well. Throw in a bit of alum as big as a walnut; this serves to make pickles hard. Skim the vinegar clean, and pour it scalding hot upon the cucumbers. Brass vessels are not healthy for preparing anything acid. Red cabbages need no other pickling than scalding, spiced vinegar poured upon them, and suffered to remain eight or ten days before you eat them. Some people think it improves them to keep them in salt and water twenty-four hours before they are pickled.

If you find your pickles soft and insipid, it is owing to the weakness of the vinegar. Throw away the vinegar, (or keep it to clean your brass kettles,) then cover your pickles with strong, scalding vinegar, into which a little all-spice, ginger, horseradish and alum have been thrown. By no means omit a pretty large bit of alum. Pickles attended to in this way, will keep for years, and be better and better every year.

Some people prefer pickled nasturtion-seed to capers. They should be kept several days after they are gathered, and then covered with boiling vinegar, and bottled when cold. They are not fit to be eaten for some months.

Martinoes are prepared in nearly the same way as other pickles. The salt and water in which they are put, two or three days previous to pickling, should be changed every day; because martinoes are very apt to become soft. No spice should be used but allspice, cloves, and cinnamon. The martinoes and the spice should be scalded *in* the vinegar, instead of pouring the vinegar *over* the martinoes.

BEER.

Beer is a good family drink. A handful of hops, to a pailful of water, and a half-pint of molasses, makes good hop beer. Spruce mixed with hops is pleasanter than hops alone. Boxberry, fever-bush, sweet fern, and horseradish make a good and healthy diet-drink. The winter evergreen, or rheumatism weed, thrown in, is very beneficial to humors. Be careful and not mistake kill-lamb for winter-evergreen ; they resemble each other. Malt mixed with a few hops makes a weak kind of beer ; but it is cool and pleasant ; it needs less molasses than hops alone. The rule is about the same for all beer. Boil the ingredients two or three hours, pour in a half-pint of molasses to a pailful, while the beer is scalding hot. Strain the beer, and when about lukewarm, put a pint of lively yeast to a barrel. Leave the bung loose till the beer is done working ; you can ascertain this by observing when the froth subsides. If your family be large, and the beer will be drank rapidly, it may as well remain in the barrel ; but if your family be small, fill what bottles you have with it ; it keeps better bottled. A raw potato or two, cut up and thrown in, while the ingredients are boiling, is said to make beer spirited.

Ginger beer is made in the following proportions :—One cup of ginger, one pint of molasses, one pail and a half of water, and a cup of lively yeast. Most people scald the ginger in half a pail of water, and then fill it up with a pailful of cold ; but in very hot weather some people stir it up cold. Yeast must not be put in till it is cold, or nearly cold. If not to be drank within twenty-four hours, it must be bottled as soon as it works.

Table beer should be drawn off into *stone* jugs, with a lump of white sugar in each, securely corked. It is brisk and pleasant, and continues good several months.

Potato cheese is much sought after in various parts of Europe. I do not know whether it is worth seeking after, or not. The following is the receipt for making :—Select good white potatoes, boil them, and, when cold, peel and reduce them to a pulp with a rasp or mortar ; to five pounds of this pulp, which must be very uniform and homogeneous, add a pint of sour milk and the requisite portion of salt; knead the whole well, cover it, and let it remain three or four days, according to the season ; then knead it afresh, and place the cheeses in small baskets, when they will part with their superfluous moisture ; dry them in the shade, and place them in layers in large pots or kegs, where they may remain a fortnight. The older they are, the finer they become.

This cheese has the advantage of never engendering worms, and of being preserved fresh for many years, provided it is kept in a dry place, and in well closed vessels.

GENERAL MAXIMS FOR HEALTH.

RISE EARLY. Eat simple food. Take plenty of exercise. Never fear a little fatigue. Let not children be dressed in tight clothes; it is necessary their limbs and muscles should have full play, if you wish for either health or beauty.

Avoid the necessity of a physician, if you can, by careful attention to your diet. Eat what best agrees with your system, and resolutely abstain from what hurts you, however well you may like it. A few days' abstinence, and cold water for a beverage, has driven off many an approaching disease.

If you find yourself really ill, send for a good physician. Have nothing to do with quacks; and do not tamper with quack medicines. You do not know what they are ; and what security have you that they know what they are?

Wear shoes that are large enough. It not only produces corns, but makes the feet misshapen, to cramp them.

Wash very often, and rub the skin thoroughly with a hard brush.

Let those who love to be invalids drink strong green tea, eat pickles, preserves, and rich pastry. As far as possible, eat and sleep at regular hours.

Wash the eyes thoroughly in cold water every morning. Do not read or sew at twilight, or by too dazzling a light. If far-sighted, read with rather less light, and with the book somewhat nearer to the eye, than you desire. If near-sighted, read with a book as far off as possible. Both these imperfections may be diminished in this way.

Clean teeth in pure water two or three times a day; but, above all, be sure to have them clean before you go to bed.

Have your bed-chamber well aired ; and have fresh bed linen every week. Never have the wind blowing directly upon you from open windows during the night. It is *not* healthy to sleep in heated rooms.

Let children have their bread and milk before they have been long up. Cold water and a run in the fresh air before breakfast.

Too frequent use of an ivory comb injures the hair. Thorough combing, washing in suds, or N. E. rum, and thorough brushing, will keep it in order ; and the washing does not injure the hair, as is generally supposed. Keep children's hair cut close until ten or twelve years old ; it is better for health and the beauty of the hair. Do not sleep with hair frizzled, or braided. Do not make children cross-eyed, by having hair hang about their foreheads, where they see it continually.

HINTS

TO

PERSONS OF MODERATE FORTUNE

[FIRST PUBLISHED IN THE MASSACHUSETTS JOURNAL.]

When clouds are seen, wise men put on their cloaks.—SHAKSPEARE.

FURNITURE.

THE prevailing evil of the present day is extravagance. I know very well that the old are too prone to preach about modern degeneracy, whether they have cause or not; but, laugh as we may at the sage advice of our fathers, it is too plain that our present expensive habits are productive of much domestic unhappiness, and injurious to public prosperity. Our wealthy people copy all the foolish and extravagant caprice of European fashion, without considering that we have not their laws of inheritance among us; and that our frequent changes of policy render property far more precarious here than in the old world. However, it is not to the rich I would speak. They have an undoubted right to spend their thousands as they please; and if they spend them ridiculously, it is consoling to reflect that they must, in some way or other, benefit the poorer classes. People of moderate fortunes have likewise an unquestioned right to dispose of their hundreds as they please; but I would ask, Is it *wise* to risk your happiness in a foolish attempt to keep up with the opulent? Of what *use* is the ef-

fort which takes so much of your time, and *all* of your in
come ? Nay, if any unexpected change in affairs should de-
prive you of a few yearly hundreds, you will find your ex-
penses have *exceeded* your income ; thus the foundation of
an accumulating debt will be laid, and your family will have
formed habits but poorly calculated to save you from the
threatened ruin. Not one valuable friend will be gained
by living beyond your means, and old age will be left to
comparative, if not to utter poverty.

There is nothing in which the extravagance of the present day strikes me so forcibly as the manner in which our
young people of moderate fortune furnish their houses.

A few weeks since, I called upon a farmer's daughter,
who had lately married a young physician of moderate tal-
ents, and destitute of fortune. Her father had given her,
at her marriage, all he ever expected to give her : viz. two
thousand dollars. Yet the lower part of her house was furnished with as much splendor as we usually find among the
wealthiest. The whole two thousand had been expended
upon Brussels carpets, alabaster vases, mahogany chairs,
and marble tables. I afterwards learned that the more
useful household utensils had been forgotten ; and that, a
few weeks after her wedding, she was actually obliged to
apply to her husband for money to purchase baskets, iron
spoons, clothes-lines, &c. ; and her husband, made irritable
by the want of money, pettishly demanded why she had
bought so many things they did not want. Did the doctor
gain any patients, or she a single friend, by offering their
visiters water in richly-cut glass tumblers, or serving them
with costly damask napkins, instead of plain soft towels ?
No ; their foolish vanity made them less happy, and no more
respectable.

Had the young lady been content with Kidderminster
carpets, and tasteful vases of her own making, she might
have put *one* thousand dollars at interest ; and had she obtained six per cent., it would have clothed her as well as
the wife of any man, who depends merely upon his own industry, ought to be clothed. This would have saved much
domestic disquiet ; for, after all, human nature is human

nature; and a wife is never better beloved, because she teases for money.

EDUCATION OF DAUGHTERS.

THERE is no subject so much connected with individual happiness and national prosperity as the education of daughters. It is a true, and therefore an old remark, that the situation and prospects of a country may be justly estimated by the character of its women; and we all know how hard it is to engraft upon a woman's character habits and principles to which she was unaccustomed in her girlish days. It is always extremely difficult, and sometimes utterly impossible. Is the present education of young ladies likely to contribute to their own ultimate happiness, or to the welfare of the country? There are many honorable exceptions; but we do think the general tone of female education is bad. The greatest and most universal error is, teaching girls to exaggerate the importance of getting married; and of course to place an undue importance upon the polite attentions of gentlemen. It was but a few days since, I heard a pretty and sensible girl say, 'Did you ever see a man so ridiculously fond of his daughters as Mr.——? He is all the time with them. The other night, at the party, I went and took Anna away by mere force; for I knew she must feel dreadfully to have her father waiting upon her all the time, while the other girls were talking with the beaux.' And another young friend of mine said, with an air most laughably serious, 'I don't think Harriet and Julia enjoyed themselves at all last night. Don't you think, nobody but their *brother* offered to hand them to the supper-room?'

That a mother should wish to see her daughters happily married, is natural and proper; that a young lady should be pleased with polite attentions is likewise natural and innocent; but this undue anxiety, this foolish excitement

about showing off the attentions of somebody, no matter
whom, is attended with consequences seriously injurious. It
promotes envy and rivalship; it leads our young girls to
spend their time between the public streets, the ball room,
and the toilet; and, worst of all, it leads them to contract
engagements, without any knowledge of their own hearts,
merely for the sake of being married as soon as their companions. When married, they find themselves ignorant of
the important duties of domestic life; and its quiet pleasures soon grow tiresome to minds worn out by frivolous
excitements. If they remain unmarried, their disappoint-
ment and discontent are, of course, in proportion to their
exaggerated idea of the eclat attendant upon having a lover. The evil increases in a startling ratio; for these girls.
so injudiciously educated, will, nine times out of ten, make
injudicious mothers, aunts, and friends; thus follies will be
accumulated unto the third and fourth generation. Young
ladies should be taught that usefulness is happiness, and
that all other things are but incidental. With regard to
matrimonial speculations, they should be taught nothing!
Leave the affections to nature and to truth, and all will
end well. How many can I at this moment recollect, who
have made themselves unhappy by marrying for the sake
of the *name* of being married! How many do I know, who
have been instructed to such watchfulness in the game, that
they have lost it by trumping their own tricks!

One great cause of the vanity, extravagance and idleness that are so fast growing upon our young ladies, is the
absence of *domestic education.* By domestic education, I
do not mean the sending daughters into the kitchen some
half dozen times, to weary the patience of the cook, and to
boast of it the next day in the parlor. I mean two or three
years spent with a mother, assisting her in her duties, in-
structing brothers and sisters, and taking care of their own
clothes. This is the way to make them happy, as well as
good wives; for, being early accustomed to the duties of
life, they will sit lightly as well as gracefully upon them.

But what time do modern girls have for the formation
of quiet, domestic habits? Until sixteen they go to school;

sometimes these years are judiciously spent, and sometimes they are half wasted ; too often they are spent in acquiring the *elements* of a thousand sciences, without being thoroughly acquainted with any ; or in a variety of accomplishments of very doubtful value to people of moderate fortune. As soon as they leave school, (and sometimes before,) they begin a round of balls and parties, and staying with gay young friends. Dress and flattery take up all their thoughts. What time have they to learn to be useful? What time have they to cultivate the still and gentle affections, which must, in every situation of life, have such an important effect on a woman's character and happiness?

As far as parents can judge what will be a daughter's station, education should be adapted to it ; but it is well to remember that it is always easy to know how to spend riches, and always safe to know how to bear poverty.

A superficial acquaintance with such accomplishments as music and drawing is useless and undesirable. They should not be attempted unless there is taste, talent, and time enough to attain excellence. I have frequently heard young women of moderate fortune say, 'I have not opened my piano these five years. I wish I had the money expended upon it. If I had employed as much time in learning useful things, I should have been better fitted for the cares of my family.'

By these remarks I do not mean to discourage an attention to the graces of life. Gentility and taste are always lovely in all situations. But good things, carried to excess, are often productive of bad consequences. When accomplishments and dress interfere with the duties and permanent happiness of life, they are unjustifiable and displeasing ; but where there is a solid foundation in mind and heart, all those elegancies are but becoming ornaments.

Some are likely to have more use for them than others ; and they are justified in spending more time and money upon them. But no one should be taught to consider them valuable for mere parade and attraction. Making the education of girls such a series of ' man-traps,' makes the whole system unhealthy, by poisoning the motive.

*　*　*　*　*　*　*　*

In tracing evils of any kind, which exist in society, we must, after all, be brought up against the great cause of all mischief—*mismanagement in education ;* and this remark applies with peculiar force to the leading fault of the present day, viz. extravagance. It is useless to expend our ingenuity in purifying the stream, unless the fountain be cleansed. If young men and young women are brought up to consider frugality contemptible, and industry degrading, it is vain to expect they will at once become prudent and useful, when the cares of life press heavily upon them. Generally speaking, when misfortune comes upon those who have been accustomed to thoughtless expenditure, it sinks them to discouragement, or, what is worse, drives them to desperation. It is true there are exceptions. There are a few, an honorable few, who, late in life, with Roman severity of resolution, learn the long-neglected lesson of economy. But how small is the number, compared with the whole mass of the population! And with what bitter agony, with what biting humiliation, is the hard lesson often learned! How easily might it have been engrafted on *early habits,* and naturally and gracefully ' grown with their growth, and strengthened with their strength !'

Yet it was but lately that I visited a family, not of 'moderate fortune,' but of no fortune at all ; one of those people who live ' nobody knows how ;' and I found a young girl, about sixteen, practising on the piano, while an elderly lady beside her was darning her stockings. I was told (for the mother was proud of bringing up her child so gen teelly) that the daughter had almost forgotten how to sew, and that a woman was hired into the house to do her mending ! ' But why,' said I, ' have you suffered your daughter to be ignorant of so useful an employment? If she is poor, the knowledge will be necessary to her ; if she is rich, it is the easiest thing in the world to lay it aside, if she chooses; she will merely be a better judge whether her work is well done by others.' ' That is true,' replied the mother ; ' and I always meant she should learn ; but she never has seemed to have any time. When she was eight years old, she could put a shirt together pretty well ; but since that, her music, and her dancing, and her school, have taken up her whole time. I did mean she should learn some domestic habits this winter ; but she has so many visiters, and is obliged to go out so much, that I suppose I must give it up. I don't like to say too much about it ; for, poor girl ! she does so love company, and she does so hate anything like care and confinement ! *Now* is her time to enjoy herself, you know. Let her take all the comfort she can, while she is single !' ' But,' said I, ' you wish her to marry some time or other ; and, in all probability, she will marry. When will she learn how to perform the duties, which are necessary and important to every mistress of a family ?' ' Oh, she will learn them when she is obliged to,' answered the injudicious mother ; ' at all events, I am determined she shall enjoy herself while she is young.'

And this is the way I have often heard mothers talk ! Yet, could parents foresee the almost inevitable consequences of such a system, I believe the weakest and vainest would abandon the false and dangerous theory. What a lesson is taught a girl in that sentence, ' *Let her enjoy herself all she can, while she is single !*' Instead of representing domestic life as the gathering place of the deepest and purest affections ; as the sphere of woman's *enjoyments* as well as of her *duties ;* as, indeed, the whole world to her ; that one pernicious sentence teaches a girl to consider matrimony desirable because ' a good match' is a triumph of vanity, and it is deemed respectable to be ' well settled in the world ;' but that it is a necessary sacrifice of her freedom and her gayety. And then how many affectionate dispositions have been trained into heartlessness, by being taught that the indulgence of indolence and vanity were necessary to their happiness ; and that to have this indulgence, they *must* marry money ! But who that marries for money, in this land of precarious fortunes, can tell how soon they will lose the glittering temptation, to which they have been willing to sacrifice so much ? And even if riches last as long as life, the evil is not remedied. Education has given a wrong end and aim to their whole existence; they have been taught to look for happiness where it never can be found, viz. in the absence of all occupation, or the unsatisfactory and ruinous excitement of fashionable competition.

The difficulty is, education does not usually point the female heart to its only true resting-place. That dear English word ' *home*,' is not half so powerful a talisman as ' *the world*.' Instead of the salutary truth, that happiness is *in* duty, they are taught to consider the two things totally distinct ; and that whoever seeks one, must sacrifice the other

The fact is, our girls have no *home education*. When quite young, they are sent to schools where no feminine employments, no domestic habits, can be learned ; and there they continue till they ' come out' into the world. After this, few find any time to arrange, and make use of, the mass of elementary knowledge they have acquired ; and fewer still have either leisure or taste for the inelegant, every-day duties of life. Thus prepared, they enter upon matrimony. Those early habits, which would have made domestic care a light and easy task, have never been taught, for fear it would interrupt their happiness ; and the result is, that when cares come, as come they must, they find them misery. I am convinced that indifference and dislike between husband and wife are more frequently occasioned by this great error in education, than by any other cause.

The bride is awakened from her delightful dream, in which carpets, vases, sofas, white gloves, and pearl earrings, are oddly jumbled up with her lover's looks and promises. Perhaps she would be surprised if she knew exactly how *much* of the fascination of being engaged was owing to the aforesaid inanimate concern. Be that as it will, she is awakened by the unpleasant conviction that cares devolve upon her. And what effect does this produce upon her character ? Do the holy and tender influences of domestic love render self-denial and exertion a bliss ? No! They would have done so, had she been *properly educated ;* but now she gives way to unavailing fretfulness and repining; and her husband is at first pained, and finally disgusted, by hearing, ' I never knew what care was when I lived in my father's house.' ' If I were to live my life over again, I would remain single as long as I could, without the risk of being an old maid.' How injudicious, how short-sighted is the policy, which thus mars the whole happiness of life, in order to make a few brief years more gay and brilliant! I have known many instances of domestic ruin and discord produced by this mistaken indulgence of mothers. *I never knew but one, where the victim had moral courage enough to change all her early habits.* She was a young, pretty, and very amiable girl ; but brought up to be perfectly useless ; a rag baby would, to all intents and purposes, have been as efficient a partner. She married a young lawyer, without property, but with good and increasing practice. She meant to be a good wife, but she did not know how. Her wastefulness involved him in debt. He did not reproach, though he tried to convince and instruct her. She loved him ; and weeping replied, ' I try to do the best I can; but when I lived at home, mother always took care of everything.' Finally, poverty came upon him ' like an armed man ;' and he went into a remote town in the Western States to teach a school. His wife folded her hands, and cried ; while he, weary and discouraged, actually came home from school to cook his own supper. At last, his patience, and her real love for him, impelled her to exertion. She promised to learn to be useful, if he would teach her. And she did learn ! And the change in her habits gradually wrought such a change in her husband's fortune, that she might bring her daughters up in idleness, had not experience taught her that economy, like grammar, is a very hard and tiresome study, after we are twenty years old.

Perhaps some will think the evils of which I have been speaking are confined principally to the rich ; but I am convinced they extend to all classes of people. All manual employment is considered degrading ; and those who are compelled to do it, try to conceal it. A few years since, very respectable young men at our colleges, cut their own wood, and blacked their own shoes. Now, how few, even of the sons of plain farmers and industrious mechanics, have moral courage enough to do without a servant; yet when they leave college, and come out into the battle of life, they *must* do without servants; and in these times it will be fortunate if one half of them get what is called ' a decent living,' even by rigid economy and patient toil. Yet I would not that servile and laborious employment should be forced upon the young. I would merely have each one educated according to his probable situation in life; and be taught that whatever is his duty, is honorable; and that no merely external circumstance can in reality injure true dignity of character. I would not cramp a boy's energies by compelling him always to cut wood, or draw water; but I would teach him not to be ashamed, should his companions happen to find him doing either one or the other. A few days since, I asked a grocer's lad to bring home some articles I had just purchased at his master's. The bundle was large; he was visibly reluctant to take it; and wished very much that I should send for it. This, however, was impossible; and he subdued his pride; but when I asked him to take back an empty bottle which belonged to the store, he, with a mortified look, begged me to do it up neatly in a paper, that it might look like a small package. Is this boy likely to be happier for cherishing a foolish pride, which will forever be jarring against his duties? Is he in reality one whit more respectable than the industrious lad who sweeps stores, or carries bottles, without troubling himself with the idea that all the world is observing his little unimportant self? For, in relation to the rest of the world, each individual is unimportant; and he alone is wise who forms his habits according to his own wants, his own prospects, and his own principles.

TRAVELLING AND PUBLIC AMUSEMENTS.

THERE is one kind of extravagance rapidly increasing in this country, which, in its effects on our purses and our *habits*, is one of the worst kinds of extravagance ; I mean the rage for travelling, and for public amusements. The good old home habits of our ancestors are breaking up—it will be well if our virtue and our freedom do not follow them ! It is easy to laugh at such prognostics,—and we are well aware that the virtue we preach is considered almost obsolete,—but let any reflecting mind inquire how decay has begun in all republics, and then let them calmly ask themselves whether we are in no danger, in departing thus rapidly from the simplicity and industry of our forefathers.

Nations do not plunge *at once* into ruin—governments do not change *suddenly*—the causes which bring about the final blow, are scarcely perceptible in the beginning ; but they increase in numbers, and in power ; they press harder and harder upon the energies and virtue of a people ; and the last steps only are alarmingly hurried and irregular. A republic without industry, economy, and integrity, is Samson shorn of his locks. A luxurious and idle *republic!* Look at the phrase !—The words were never made to be married together ; every body sees it would be death to one of them.

And are not *we* becoming luxurious and idle ? Look at our steamboats, and stages, and taverns ! There you will find mechanics, who have left debts and employment to take care of themselves, while they go to take a peep at the great canal, or the opera-dancers. There you will find domestics all agog for their wages-worth of travelling ; why should they look out for ' a rainy day ?' There are hospitals enough to provide for them in sickness ; and as for marrying, they have no idea of that, till they can find a man who will support them genteelly. There you will find mothers, who have left the children at home with Betsey, while they go to improve their minds at the Mountain House, or the Springs.

If only the rich did this, all would be well. They benefit others, and do not injure themselves. In any situation,
idleness is their curse, and uneasiness is the tax they must
pay for affluence ; but their restlessness is as great a benefit to the community as the motions of Prince Esterhazy,
when at every step the pearls drop from his coat.

People of moderate fortune have just as good a right to
travel as the wealthy ; but is it not unwise ? Do they not
injure themselves and their families ? You say travelling
is cheap. So is staying at home. Besides, do you count
all the costs ?

The money you pay for stages and steamboats is the
smallest of the items. There are clothes bought which
would not otherwise be bought ; those clothes are worn
out and defaced twenty times as quick as they would have
been at home ; children are perhaps left with domestics, or
strangers ; their health and morals, to say the least, under
very uncertain influence ; your substance is wasted in your
absence by those who have no self-interest to prompt them
to carefulness ; you form an acquaintance with a multitude
of people, who will be sure to take your house in their
way, when they travel next year ; and finally, you become
so accustomed to excitement, that home appears insipid,
and it requires no small effort to return to the quiet routine
of your duties. And what do you get in return for all this ?
Some pleasant scenes, which will soon seem to you like a
dream ; some pleasant faces, which you will never see
again ; and much of crowd, and toil, and dust, and bustle.

I once knew a family which formed a striking illustration
of my remarks. The man was a farmer, and his wife was
an active, capable woman, with more of ambition than
sound policy. Being in debt, they resolved to take fashionable boarders from Boston, during the summer season.
These boarders, at the time of their arrival, were project-
ing a jaunt to the Springs ; and they talked of Lake George
crystals, and Canadian music, and English officers, and
' dark blue Ontario,' with its beautiful little brood of *lake-
lets,* as Wordsworth would call them ; and how one lady
was dressed superbly at Saratoga ; and how another was

scandalized for always happening to drop her fan in the vicinity of the wealthiest beaux. All this fired the quiet imagination of the good farmer's wife; and no sooner had the boarders departed to enjoy themselves in spite of heat, and dust, and fever-and-ague, than she stated her determination to follow them. 'Why have we not as good a right to travel, as they have?' said she; 'they have paid us money enough to go to Niagara with; and it really is a shame for people to live and die so ignorant of their own country.' 'But then we want the money to pay for that stock, which turned out unlucky, you know.' 'Oh, that can be done next summer; we can always get boarders enough, and those that will pay handsomely. Give the man a mortgage of the house, to keep him quiet till next summer.' 'But what will you do with the children?' 'Sally is a very smart girl; I am sure she will take as good care of them as if I were at home.'

To make a long story short, the farmer and his wife concluded to go to Quebec, just to show they had a *right* to put themselves to inconvenience, if they pleased. They went; spent all their money; had a watch stolen from them in the steamboat; were dreadfully sea-sick off Point Judith; came home tired, and dusty; found the babe sick, because Sally had stood at the door with it, one chilly, damp morning, while she was feeding the chickens; and the eldest girl screaming and screeching at the thoughts of going to bed, because Sally, in order to bring her under her authority, had told her a frightful ' raw-head-and-bloody-bones' story; the horse had broken into the garden, and made wretched work with the vegetables; and fifty pounds of butter had become fit for the grease-pot, because the hoops of the firkin had sprung, and Sally had so much to do, that she never thought of going to see whether the butter was covered with brine.

After six or eight weeks, the children were pretty well restored to orderly habits; and the wife, being really a notable and prudent woman, resolved to make up for her lost butter and vegetables, by doing without help through the winter. When summer came, they should have boarders,

she said ; and sure enough, they had boarders in plenty ;
but not profitable ones.   There were forty cousins, at
whose houses they had stopped ; and twenty people who had
been very polite to them on the way ; and it being such a
pleasant season, and *travelling so cheap*, every one of these
people felt they had *a right* to take a journey ; and they
could not help passing a day or two with their friends at
the farm.   One after another came, till the farmer could
bear it no longer.   ' I tell you what, wife,' said he, ' I am
going to jail as fast as a man can go.   If there is no other
way of putting a stop to this, I'll sell every bed in the house,
except the one we sleep on.'

And sure enough, he actually did this ; and when the
forty-first cousin came down on a friendly visit, on account
of what her other cousins had told her about the cheapness
of travelling, she was told they should be very happy to
sleep on the floor, for the sake of accommodating her, for
a night or two ; but the truth was, they had but one bed in
the house.   This honest couple are now busy in paying
off their debts, and laying by something for their old age.
He facetiously tells how he went to New York to have his
watch stolen, and his boots blacked like a looking glass ;
and she shows her Lake George diamond ring, and tells how
the steamboat was crowded, and how afraid she was the
boiler would burst, and always ends by saying, ' After all, it
was a toil of pleasure.'

However, it is not our farmers, who are in the greatest
danger of this species of extravagance ; for we look to that
class of people, as the strongest hold of republican simplicity, industry, and virtue.   It is from adventurers, swindlers,
broken down traders,—all that rapidly increasing class of
idlers, too genteel to work, and too proud to beg,—that
we have most reason to dread examples of extravagance.
A very respectable tavern-keeper has lately been driven
to establish a rule, that no customer shall be allowed to
rise from the table till he pays for his meal.   ' I know it is
rude to give such orders to honest men,' said he, ' and
three years ago I would as soon cut off my hand as have
done it ; but now, travelling is so cheap, that all sorts of

characters are on the move; and I find more than half of them will get away, if they can, without paying a cent.'

With regard to public amusements, it is still worse. Rope-dancers, and opera-dancers, and all sorts of dancers, go through the country, making thousands as they go; while, from high to low, there is one universal, despairing groan of 'hard times,' 'dreadful gloomy times!'

These things ought not to be. People who have little to spend, should partake sparingly of useless amusements; those who are in debt should deny themselves entirely. Let me not be supposed to inculcate exclusive doctrines. I would have every species of enjoyment as open to the poor as to the rich; but I would have people consider well how they are likely to obtain the greatest portion of happiness, taking the whole of their lives into view; I would not have them sacrifice permanent respectability and comfort to present gentility and love of excitement; above all, I caution them to beware that this love of excitement does not grow into a habit, till the fireside becomes a dull place, and the gambling table and the bar-room finish what the theatre began.

If men would have women economical, they must be so themselves. What motive is there for patient industry, and careful economy, when the savings of a month are spent at one trip to Nahant, and more than the value of a much desired, but rejected dress, is expended during the stay of a new set of comedians? We make a great deal of talk about being republicans; if we are so in reality, we shall stay at home, to mind our business, and educate our children, so long as one or the other need our attention, or can suffer by our neglect.

PHILOSOPHY AND CONSISTENCY.

AMONG all the fine things Mrs. Barbauld wrote, she never wrote anything better than her essay on the Inconsistency of Human Expectations. ' Everything,' says she, ' is marked at a settled price. Our time, our labor, our ingenuity, is so much ready money, which we are to lay out to the best advantage. Examine, compare, choose, reject; but stand to your own judgment; and do not, like children, when you have purchased one thing, repine that you do not possess another, which you would not purchase. Would you be rich? Do you think *that* the single point worth sacrificing everything else to? You may then be rich. Thousands have become so from the lowest beginnings by toil, and diligence, and attention to the minutest articles of expense and profit. But you must give up the pleasures of leisure, of an unembarrassed mind, and of a free, unsuspicious temper. You must learn to do hard, if not unjust things; and as for the embarrassment of a delicate and ingenuous spirit, it is necessary for you to get rid of it as fast as possible. You must not stop to enlarge your mind, polish your taste, or refine your sentiments; but must keep on in one beaten track, without turning aside to the right hand or the left. " But," you say, " I cannot submit to drudgery like this; I feel a spirit above it." 'Tis well; be above it then ; only do not repine because you are not rich. Is knowledge the pearl of price in your estimation? That too may be purchased by steady application, and long, solitary hours of study and reflection. " But," says the man of letters, " what a hardship is it that many an illiterate fellow, who cannot construe the motto on his coach, shall raise a fortune, and make a figure, while I possess merely the common conveniences of life." Was it for fortune, then, that you grew pale over the midnight lamp, and gave the sprightly years of youth to study and reflection? You then have mistaken your path, and ill employed your industry. " What reward have I then for all my labor?" What reward! A large comprehensive soul, purged from vulgar fears and prejudices, able to interpret the works of man and God. A perpetual spring of fresh ideas, and the conscious dignity of superior intelligence. Good Heaven! what other reward can you ask! "But is it not a reproach upon the economy of Providence that such a one, who is a mean, dirty fellow, should have amassed wealth enough to buy half a nation?" Not in the least. He made himself a mean, dirty fellow, for that very end. He has paid his health, his conscience, and his liberty for it. Do you envy him his bargain? Will you hang your head in his presence, because he outshines you in equipage and show? Lift up your brow with a noble confidence, and say to yourself, "I have not these things, it is true; but it is because I have not desired, or sought them; it is because I possess something better. I have chosen my lot! I am content, and satisfied." The most characteristic mark of a great mind is to choose some one object, which it considers important, and pursue that object through life. If we expect the purchase, we must pay the price.'

'There is a pretty passage in one of Lucian's dialogues, where Jupiter complains to Cupid, that, though he has had so many intrigues, he was never sincerely beloved. "In order to be loved," says Cupid, "you must lay aside your ægis and your thunder-bolts; you must curl and perfume your hair, and place a garland on your head, and walk with a soft step, and assume a winning, obsequious deportment." "But," replied Jupiter, "I am not willing to resign so much of my dignity." "Then," returned Cupid, "leave off desiring to be loved."'

These remarks by Mrs. Barbauld are full of sound philosophy. Who has not observed, in his circle of acquaintance, and in the recesses of his own heart, the same inconsistency of expectation, the same peevishness of discontent.

Says Germanicus, 'There is my dunce of a classmate has found his way into Congress, and is living amid the perpetual excitement of intellectual minds, while I am cooped up in an ignorant country parish, obliged to be at

the beck and call of every old woman, who happens to feel
uneasy in her mind.'

'Well, Germanicus, the road to political distinction was
as open to you as to him; why did you not choose it?'
'Oh, I could not consent to be the tool of a party; to shake
hands with the vicious, and flatter fools. It would gall me
to the quick to hear my opponents accuse me of actions I
never committed, and of motives which worlds would not
tempt me to indulge.' Since Germanicus is wise enough
to know the whistle costs more than it is worth, is he not
unreasonable to murmur because he has not bought it?

Matrona always wears a discontented look when she
hears the praises of Clio. 'I used to write her composition
for her, when we were at school together,' says she; 'and
now she is quite the idol of the literary world; while I am
never heard of beyond my own family, unless some one
happens to introduce me as the friend of Clio.' 'Why
not write, then; and see if the world will not learn to introduce Clio as the friend of Matrona?' 'I write! not for the
world! I could not endure to pour my soul out to an un-
discerning multitude; I could not see my cherished
thoughts caricatured by some soulless reviewer, and my
favorite fancies expounded by the matter-of-fact editor of
some stupid paper.' Why does Matrona envy what she
knows costs so much, and is of so little value?

Yet so it is, through all classes of society. All of us cov-
et some neighbor's possession, and think our lot would
have been happier, had it been different from what it is.
Yet most of us could obtain worldly distinctions, if our habits and inclinations allowed us to pay the immense price at
which they must be purchased. True wisdom lies in finding out all the advantages of a situation in which we *are*
placed, instead of imagining the enjoyments of one in which
we are *not* placed.

Such philosophy is rarely found. The most perfect
sample I ever met was an old woman, who was apparent-
ly the poorest and most forlorn of the human species—so
true is the maxim which all profess to believe, and which
none act upon invariably, viz. that happiness does not de-

pend on outward circumstances. The wise woman, to
whom I have alluded, *walks* to Boston, from a distance of
twenty-five or thirty miles, to sell a bag of brown thread and
stockings; and then patiently foots it back again with her
little gains.   Her dress, though tidy, is a grotesque collection of ' shreds and patches,' coarse in the extreme.   ' Why
don't you come down in a wagon?' said I, when I observed that she was soon to become a mother, and was evi-
dently wearied with her long journey.   ' We h'an't got any
horse,' replied she; ' the neighbors are very kind to me,
but they can't spare their'n ; and it would cost as much to
hire one, as all my thread will come to.' ' You have a
husband—don't he do anything for you.' ' He is a good
man; he does all he can ; but he's a cripple and an invalid.   He reels my yarn, and *specks* the children's shoes.
He's as kind a husband as a woman need to have.' ' But
his being a cripple is a heavy misfortune to you,' said I.
' Why, ma'am, I don't look upon it in that light,' replied
the thread-woman; ' I consider that I've great reason to
be thankful he never took to any bad habits.' ' How many children have you?'   ' Six sons, and five *darters*,
ma'am.' ' Six sons and five daughters ! What a family
for a poor woman to support !' ' It's a family, surely,
ma'am; but there an't one of 'em I'd be willing to lose.
They are as good children as need to be—all willing to
work, and all clever to me.   Even the littlest boy, when
he gets a cent now and then for doing a *chore*, will be sure
and bring it to ma'am.' ' Do your daughters spin your
thread ?' ' No, ma'am ; as soon as they are old enough,
they go out to *sarvice*.   I don't want to keep them always
delving for me; they are always willing to give me what
they can ; but it is right and fair they should do a little for
themselves.   I do all my spinning after the folks are abed.'
' Don't you think you should be better off, if you had no
one but yourself to provide for ?' ' Why, no, ma'am, I don't.
If I had'nt been married, I should always have had to work
as hard as I could ; and now I can't do more than that.
My children are a great comfort to me ; and I look forward

to the time when they'll do as much for me as I have done
for them.'

Here was true philosophy! I learned a lesson from that
poor woman which I shall not soon forget. If I wanted
true, hearty, well principled service, I would employ children brought up by such a mother.

REASONS FOR HARD TIMES.

PERHAPS there never was a time when the depressing
effects of stagnation in business were so universally felt, all
the world over, as they are now.—The merchant sends
out old dollars, and is lucky if he gets the same number
of new ones in return ; and he who has a share in manu-
factures, has bought a 'bottle imp,' which he will do well
to hawk about the street for the lowest possible coin. The
effects of this depression must of course be felt by all
grades of society. Yet who that passes through Cornhill at
one o'clock, and sees the bright array of wives and daughters, as various in their decorations as the insects, the birds
and the shells, would believe that the community was stag-
gering under a weight which almost paralyzes its move-
ments? 'Everything is so cheap,' say the ladies, 'that, it
is inexcusable not to dress well.' But do they reflect *why*
things are so cheap? Do they know how much wealth has
been sacrificed, how many families ruined, to produce this
boasted result? Do they not know enough of the machin-
ery of society, to suppose that the stunning effect of crash
after crash, may eventually be felt by those on whom they
depend for support?

Luxuries are cheaper now than necessaries were a few
years since : yet it is a lamentable fact, that it costs more
to live now than it did formerly. When silk was nine shillings per yard, seven or eight yards sufficed for a dress ;

now it is four or five shillings, sixteen or twenty yards will hardly satisfy the mantuamaker.

If this extravagance were confined to the wealthiest classes, it would be productive of more good than evil. But if the rich have a new dress every fortnight, people of moderate fortune will have one every month. In this way, finery becomes the standard of respectability; and a man's cloth is of more consequence than his character.

Men of fixed salaries spend every cent of their income, and then leave their children to depend on the precarious charity and reluctant friendship of a world they have wasted their substance to please. Men who rush into enterprise and speculation, keep up their credit by splendor; and should they sink, they and their families carry with them extravagant habits to corrode their spirits with discontent, perchance to tempt them into crime. ' I know we are extravagant,' said one of my acquaintance, the other day; ' but how can I help it? My husband does not like to see his wife and daughters dress more meanly than those with whom they associate.' ' Then, my dear lady, your husband has not as much moral dignity and moral courage as I thought he had. He should be content to see his wife and daughters respected for neatness, good taste, and attractive manners.' ' This all sounds very well in talk,' replied the lady; ' but, say what you will about pleasing and intelligent girls, nobody will attend to them unless they dress in the fashion. If my daughters were to dress in the plain, neat style you recommend, they would see all their acquaintance asked to dance more frequently than themselves, and not a gentleman would join them in Cornhill.'

' I do not believe this in so extensive a sense as you do. Girls may appear genteelly without being extravagant, and though some fops may know the most approved color for a ribbon, or the newest arrangement for trimming, I believe gentlemen of real character merely notice whether a lady's dress is generally in good taste, or not. But, granting your statement to be true, in its widest sense, of what consequence is it? How much will the whole happiness of your daughter's life be affected by her dancing some fifty times less than her companions, or wasting some few hours less in the empty conversation of coxcombs? A man often admires a style of dress, which he would not venture to support in a wife. Extravagance has prevented many marriages, and rendered still more unhappy. And should your daughters fail in forming good connexions, what have you to leave them, save extravagant habits, too deeply rooted to be eradicated. Think you those who now laugh at them for a soiled glove, or an unfashionable ribbon, will assist their poverty, or cheer their neglected old age? No; they would find them as cold and selfish as they are vain. A few thousands in the bank are worth all the fashionable friends in Christendom.'

Whether my friend was convinced, or not, I cannot say; but I saw her daughters in Cornhill, the next week, with new French hats and blonde veils.

It is really melancholy to see how this fever of extravagance rages, and how it is sapping the strength of our happy country. It has no bounds; it pervades all ranks, and characterizes all ages.

I know the wife of a pavier, who spends her three hundred a year in ' outward adorning,' and who will not condescend to speak to her husband, while engaged in his honest calling.

Mechanics, who should have too high a sense of their own respectability to resort to such pitiful competition, will indulge their daughters in dressing like the wealthiest; and a domestic would certainly leave you, should you dare advise her to lay up one cent of her wages.

'These things ought not to be.' Every man and every woman should lay up some portion of their income, whether that income be great or small.

HOW TO ENDURE POVERTY.

THAT a thorough, religious, *useful* education is the best security against misfortune, disgrace and poverty, is universally believed and acknowledged; and to this we add the firm conviction, that, when poverty comes (as it sometimes will) upon the prudent, the industrious, and the well-informed, a judicious education is all-powerful in enabling them to *endure* the evils it cannot always *prevent*. A mind full of piety and knowledge is always rich; it is a bank that never fails; it yields a perpetual dividend of happiness.

In a late visit to the alms-house at ——, we saw a remarkable evidence of the truth of this doctrine. Mrs. —— was early left an orphan. She was educated by an uncle and aunt, both of whom had attained the middle age of life. Theirs was an industrious, well-ordered, and cheerful family. Her uncle was a man of sound judgment, liberal feelings, and great knowledge of human nature. This he showed by the education of the young people under his care. He allowed them to waste no time; every moment must be spent in learning something, or in doing something. He encouraged an entertaining, lively style of conversation, but discountenanced all remarks about persons, families, dress, and engagements; he used to say, parents were not aware how such topics frittered away the minds of young people, and what inordinate importance they learned to attach to them, when they heard them constantly talked about.

In his family, Sunday was a happy day; for it was made a day of religious instruction, without any unnatural constraint upon the gayety of the young. The Bible was the text book; the places mentioned in it were traced on maps; the manners and customs of different nations were explained; curious phenomena in the natural history of those countries were read; in a word, everything was done to cherish a spirit of humble, yet earnest inquiry. In this excellent family Mrs.——remained till her marriage. In the course of fifteen years, she lost her uncle, her aunt, and her husband. She was left destitute, but supported herself comfortably by her own exertions, and retained the respect and admiration of a large circle of friends. Thus she passed her life in cheerfulness and honor during ten years; at the end of that time, her humble residence took fire from an adjoining house in the night time, and she escaped by jumping from the chamber window. In consequence of the injury received by this fall, her right arm was amputated, and her right leg became entirely useless. Her friends were very kind and attentive; and for a short time she consented to live on their bounty; but, aware that the claims on private charity are very numerous, she, with the genuine independence of a strong mind, resolved to avail herself of the public provision for the helpless poor. The name of going to the alms-house had nothing terrifying or disgraceful to *her ;* for she had been taught that *conduct* is the real standard of respectability. She is there, with a heart full of thankfulness to the Giver of all things; she is patient, pious, and uniformly cheerful. She instructs the young, encourages the old, and makes herself delightful to all, by her various knowledge and entertaining conversation. Her character reflects dignity on her situation; and those who visit the establishment, come away with sentiments of respect and admiration for this voluntary resident of the alms-house.

*   *   *   *   *   *   *   *

What a contrast is afforded by the character of the woman who occupies the room next hers! She is so indolent and filthy, that she can with difficulty be made to attend to her own personal comfort; and even the most patient are worn out with her perpetual fretfulness. Her mind is continually infested with envy, hatred, and discontent. She thinks Providence has dealt hardly with her; that all the world are proud and ungrateful; and that every one despises her because she is in the alms-house. This pitiable state of mind is the natural result of her education.

Her father was a respectable mechanic, and might have been a wealthy one, had he not been fascinated by the beauty of a thoughtless, idle, showy girl, whom he made his wife. The usual consequences followed—he could not earn money so fast as she could spend it; the house became a scene of discord ; the daughter dressed in the fashion ; learned to play on the piano; was taught to think that being engaged in any useful employment was very ungenteel; and that to be *engaged to be married* was the chief end and aim of woman; the father died a bankrupt; the weak and frivolous mother lingered along in beggary, for a while, and then died of vexation and shame.

The friends of the family were very kind to the daughter ; but her extreme indolence, her vanity, pertness, and ingratitude, finally exhausted the kindness of the most generous and forbearing ; and as nothing could induce her to personal exertion, she was at length obliged to take shelter in the alms-house. Here her misery is incurable. She has so long been accustomed to think dress and parade the necessary elements of happiness, that she despises all that is done for her comfort; her face has settled into an expression which looks like an imbodied growl; every body is tired of listening to her complaints; and even the little children run away, when they see her coming.

May not those who have children to educate, learn a good lesson from these women ? Those who have wealth, have recently had many and bitter lessons to prove how suddenly riches may take to themselves wings ; and those who *certainly* have but little to leave, should indeed beware how they bestow upon their children, the accursed inheritance of indolent and extravagant habits.

APPENDIX

TO THE

AMERICAN FRUGAL HOUSEWIFE.

Those sentences marked with a star relate to subjects mentioned in other parts of the book.

TO PRESERVE GREEN CURRANTS.—Currants may be kept fresh for a year or more, if they are gathered when green, separated from the stems, put into dry, clean junk bottles, and corked very carefully, so as to exclude the air. They should be kept in a cool place in the cellar.

CANDLES.—Very hard and durable candles are made in the following manner: Melt together ten ounces of mutton tallow, a quarter of an ounce of camphor, four ounces of beeswax, and two ounces of alum. Candles made of these materials burn with a very clear light.

*VARNISHED FURNITURE.—If you wish to give a fine soft polish to varnished furniture, and remove any slight imperfections, rub it once or twice a week with pulverized rotten-stone and linseed oil, and afterward wipe clean with a soft silk rag.

CREAM.—The quantity of cream on milk may be greatly increased by the following process: Have two pans ready in boiling hot water, and when the new milk is brought in, put it into one of these hot pans and cover it with the other. The quality as well as the thickness of the cream is improved.

*TEETH.—Honey mixed with pure pulverized charcoal is said to be excellent to cleanse the teeth, and make them white. Lime-water with a little Peruvian bark is very good to be occasionally used by those who have defective teeth, or an offensive breath.

TAINTED BUTTER.—Some good cooks say that bad butter may be purified in the following manner: Melt and skim it, then put into it a piece of *well-toasted* bread; in a few minutes the butter will lose its offensive taste and smell; the bread will absorb it all. Slices of potato fried in rancid lard will in a great measure absorb the unpleasant taste.

TOMATOES PIE.—Tomatoes make excellent pies. Skins taken

off with scalding water, stewed twenty minutes or more, salted, prepared the same as rich squash pies, only an egg or two more.

*It is a great improvement to the flavor of PUMPKIN PIES to boil the milk, stir the sifted pumpkin into it, and let them boil up together once or twice. The pumpkin swells almost as much as Indian meal, and of course absorbs more milk than when stirred together cold; but the taste of the pie is much improved.

Some people cut pumpkin, string it, and dry it like apples. It is a much better way to boil and sift the pumpkin, then spread it out thin in tin plates, and dry hard in a warm oven. It will keep good all' the year round, and a little piece boiled up in milk will make a batch of pies.

*Most people think BRASS KETTLES for washing are not as likely to collect verdigris, if they are never cleaned in any other way than by washing in strong soap suds just before they are used.

INK SPOTS.—If soaked in warm milk before the ink has a chance to dry, the spot may usually be removed. If it has dried in, rub table-salt upon it, and drop lemon-juice upon the salt. This answers nearly as well as the salts of lemon sold by apothecaries. If a lemon cannot be easily procured, vinegar, or sorrel-juice, will answer. White soap diluted with vinegar is likewise a good thing to take out ink spots.

STARCH.—Frozen potatoes yield more flour for starch than fresh ones. The frost may be taken out by soaking them in cold water a few hours before cooking; if frozen very hard, it may be useful to throw a little saltpetre into the water.

FEATHERS.—It is said that tumbled plumes may be restored to elasticity and beauty by dipping them in hot water, then shaking and drying them.

ICY STEPS.—Salt strewed upon the door-steps in winter will cause the ice to crack, so that it can be easily removed.

FLOWERS.—Flowers may be preserved fresh in tumblers or vases by putting a handful of salt in the water, to increase its coldness.

WHITE-WASHING is said to last longer if the new-slaked lime be mixed with skim-milk.

HORSE-FLIES.—Indigo-weed stuck plentifully about the harness tends to keep flies from horses. Some make a decoction of indigo-weed, and others of pennyroyal, and bathe horses with it, to defend them from insects.

PINE APPLES will keep much better if the green crown at top

be twisted off. The vegetation of the crown takes the goodness from the fruit, n the same way that sprouts injure vegetables. The crown can be stuck on for ornament, if necessary.

*THE PILES.—Those who have tried other remedies for this disorder in vain, have found relief from the following medicine : Stew a handful of low mallows in about three gills of milk ; strain it, and mix about half the quantity of West India molasses with it. As warm as is agreeable.

WARTS.—It is said that if the top of a wart be wet and rubbed two or three times a day with a piece of unslaked lime, it cures the wart soon, and leaves no scar.

*CANCERS.—The Indians have great belief in the efficacy of poultices of stewed cranberries, for the relief of *cancers*. They apply them fresh and warm every ten or fifteen minutes, night and day. Whether this will effect a cure I know not ; I simply know that the Indians strongly recommend it. Salts, or some simple physic, is taken every day during the process.

EAR-WAX.—Nothing is better than ear-wax to prevent the painful effects resulting from a wound by a nail, skewer, &c. It should be put on as soon as possible. Those who are troubled with cracked lips have found this remedy successful when others have failed. It is one of those sorts of cures, which are very likely to be laughed at ; but I know of its having produced very beneficial results.

*BURNS.—If a person who is burned will *patiently* hold the injured part in water, it will prevent the formation of a blister. If the water be too cold, it may be slightly warmed, and produce the same effect. People in general are not willing to try it for a sufficiently long time. Chalk and hog's lard simmered together are said to make a good ointment for a burn.

*BRUISES.—Constant application of warm water is very soothing to bruised flesh, and may serve to prevent bad consequences while other things are in preparation.

SORE NIPPLES.—Put twenty grains of sugar of lead into a vial with one gill of rose-water ; shake it up thoroughly ; wet a piece of soft linen with this preparation, and put it on ; renew this as often as the linen becomes dry. Before nursing, wash this off with something soothing ; rose-water is very good ; but the best thing is quince-seed warmed in a little cold tea until the liquid becomes quite glutinous. This application is alike healing and pleasant.

A raw onion is an excellent remedy for the STING OF A WASP.

Corns.—A corn may be extracted from the foot by binding on half a raw cranberry, with the cut side of the fruit upon the foot. I have known a very old and troublesome corn drawn out in this way, in the course of a few nights.

Heart-Burn.—Eat magnesia for the heart-burn.

Chloride of Lime.—A room may be purified from offensive smells of any kind by a few spoonsful of chloride of lime dissolved in water. A good-sized saucer, or some similar vessel, is large enough for all common purposes. The article is cheap, and is invaluable in the apartment of an invalid.

Eggs in Winter.—The reason hens do not usually lay eggs in the winter is that the gravel is covered up with snow, and therefore they are not furnished with lime to form the shells. If the bones left of meat, poultry, &c. are pounded and mixed with their food, or given to them alone, they will eat them very eagerly, and will lay eggs the same as in summer. Hens fed on oats are much more likely to lay well than those fed on corn.

Pearls.—In order to preserve the beauty of pearl ornaments, they should be carefully kept from dampness. A piece of paper torn off and rolled up, so as to present a soft, ragged edge, is the best thing to cleanse them with.

Varnishing Gilded Frames.—It is said that looking-glass frames may be cleansed with a damp cloth, without injury, provided they are varnished with the *pure white alcoholic varnish*, used for transferred engravings and other delicate articles of fancy-work. This would save the trouble of covering and uncovering picture-frames with the change of the seasons. I never heard how many coats of varnish were necessary, but I should think it would be safe to put on more than one.

Cologne Water.—One pint of alcohol, sixty drops of lavender, sixty drops of bergamot, sixty drops of essence of lemon, sixty drops of orange water. To be corked up, and well shaken. It is better for considerable age.

Grease Spots.—Magnesia rubbed upon the spot, covered with clean paper, and a warm iron placed above, will usually draw out grease. Where a considerable quantity of oil has been spilled. it will be necessary to repeat the operation a great many times, in order to extract it all.

Receipt for making excellent Bread without Yeast.— Scald about two handsful of Indian meal, into which put a little salt, and as much cold water as will make it rather warmer than new milk ; then stir in wheat flour, till it is as thick as a family pudding, and set it down by the fire to rise. In about half an hour, it generally grows thin; you may sprinkle a little fresh flour on the top, and mind to turn the pot round, that it may not bake to the side of it. In three or four hours, if you mind the above directions, it will rise and ferment as if you had set it with hop yeast ; when it does, make it up in soft dough, flour a pan, put in your bread, set it before the fire, covered up, turn it round to make it equally warm, and in about half an hour it will be light enough to bake. It suits best to bake in a Dutch oven, as it should be put into the oven as soon as it is light.

RICE JELLY.—Boil a quarter of a pound of rice flour with half a pound of loaf sugar, in a quart of water, till the whole becomes one glutinous mass, then strain off the jelly and let it stand to cool. This food is very nourishing and beneficial to invalids.

APPLE MARMALADE.—Scald apples till they will pulp from the core ; take an equal weight of sugar in large lumps, and boil it in just water enough to dip the lumps well, until it can be skimmed, and is a thick syrup ; mix this with the apple pulp, and simmer it on a quick fire for fifteen minutes. Keep it in pots covered with paper dipped in brandy.

QUINCE MARMALADE.—To two pounds of quince put three quarters of a pound of nice sugar, and a pint of spring water. Boil them till they are tender; then take them up and bruise them ; again put them in the liquor, and let them boil three quarters of an hour, then put it into jars, covered as mentioned above. Those who like things very sweet put an equal quantity of quince and sugar ; but I think the flavor is less delicious.

RASPBERRY JAM.—Take an equal quantity of fruit and sugar. Put the raspberries into a pan, boil and stir them constantly till juicy and well broken ; add as much sugar, boil and skim it till it is reduced to a fine jam. Put it away in the same manner as other preserves.

BLANC-MANGER.—Boil two ounces of isinglass in one pint and a half of new milk ; strain it into one pint of thick cream. Sweeten it to your taste, add one cup of rose-water, boil it up once, let it settle, and put it in your moulds.

Some prefer to boil two ounces of isinglass in three and a half pints of water for half an hour, then strain it to one pint and a half of cream, sweeten it, add a teacup of rose-water, and boil up once.

Isinglass is the most expensive ingredient in blanc-manger. Some decidedly prefer the jelly of calves' feet. The jelly is obtained by boiling four feet in a gallon of water till reduced to a quart, strained, cooled, and skimmed. A pint of jelly to a pint of cream; in other respects done the same as isinglass blanc-manger. Some boil a stick of cinnamon, or a grated lemon-peel, in the jelly. The moulds should be made thoroughly clean, and wet with cold water; the white of an egg, dropped in and shook round the moulds, will make it come out smooth and handsomely.

PORK JELLY.—Some people like the jelly obtained from a boiled hand of pork, or the feet of pork, prepared in the same way as calf's-foot jelly; for which see page 31.

The cloths, or jelly-bags, through which jelly is strained, should be first wet to prevent waste.

CRANBERRY JELLY.—Mix isinglass jelly, or calf's-foot jelly, with a double quantity of cranberry juice, sweeten it with fine loaf sugar, boil it up once, and strain it to cool.

RICH CUSTARDS.—Boil a pint of milk with lemon-peel and a stick of cinnamon. While it is boiling, beat up the yolks of five eggs with a pint of cream. When the milk tastes of the spice, pour it to the cream, stirring well; sweeten it to taste. Give the custard a simmer, till of a proper thickness, but do not let it boil. Stir the whole time one way. Season it with a little rose-water, and a few spoonsful of wine or brandy, as you may prefer. When put into cups, grate on nutmeg.

TO PRESERVE PEACHES.—Scald peaches in boiling water, but do not let them boil; take them out and put them in cold water, then dry them in a sieve, and put them in long, wide-mouthed bottles. To a half dozen peaches put a quarter of a pound of clarified sugar; pour it over the peaches, fill up the bottles with brandy, and stop them close.

COCOA-NUT CAKES.—Grate the meat of two cocoa-nuts, after pealing off the dark skin; allow an equal weight of loaf sugar, pounded and sifted, and the rind and juice of two lemons. Mix the ingredients well; make into cakes about as big as a nutmeg, with a little piece of citron in each. Bake them on buttered tin sheets about twenty minutes, in a moderately hot oven.

*TO CLARIFY SUGAR.—Put half a pint of water to a pound of sugar; whip up the white of an egg and stir it in, and put it over the fire. When it first boils up, check it with a little cold water; the second time set it away to cool. In a quarter of an hour, skim the top, and turn the syrup off quickly, so as to leave the sediment which will collect at the bottom.

*RICH WEDDING CAKE.—One pound three quarters of flour, one pound one quarter of butter, do. of sugar, one dozen eggs, two pounds of currants, one gill of wine, half a gill of brandy, one pound of citron, cut in slices, a wine-glass of rose-water, three quarters of an ounce of nutmeg, quarter of an ounce of cloves, the same of allspice. The rind of two lemons grated in. See page 72 for baking.

STILL RICHER WEDDING CAKE.—Three pounds of flour, three pounds of butter, three pounds of sugar, twenty-eight eggs, six pounds of currants, and six pounds of seeded raisins ; one ounce of cinnamon, one ounce of nutmeg, three quarters of an ounce of cloves, half an ounce of mace, one pound of citron, two glasses of brandy, two glasses of rose-water, and one glass of wine. For baking, see page 72.

*FROSTING FOR CAKE.—It is a great improvement to squeeze r little lemon-juice into the egg and sugar prepared for frosting It gives a fine flavor, and makes it extremely white. For frosting, see directions, page 72.

WHIP SYLLABUB.—One pint of cream, one pint of wine, the juice and grated peel of a lemon, and the white of two eggs; sweeten it to your taste, put it into a deep vessel, and whip it to a light froth. Fill your glasses with the froth as it rises. It is a good plan to put some of the froth in a sieve, over a dish, and have it in readiness to heap upon the top of your glasses after you have filled them. Some people put a spoonful of marmalade or jelly at the bottom of the glasses, before they are filled.

LOBSTER SALAD.—The meat of one lobster is extracted from the shell, and cut up fine. Have fresh hard lettuce cut up very fine ; mix it with the lobster. Make a dressing, in a deep plate, of the yolks of four eggs cut up, a gill of sweet oil, a gill of vinegar, half a gill of mustard, half a teaspoonful of cayenne, half a teaspoonful of salt ; all mixed well together. To be prepared just before eaten. Chicken salad is prepared in the same way, only chicken is used instead of lobster, and celery instead of lettuce.

ESCALOPED OYSTERS.—Put crumbled bread around the sides and bottom of a buttered dish. Put oysters in a skillet, and let the heat just strike them through; then take them out of the shells, and rinse them thoroughly in the water they have stewed in. Put half of them on the layer of crumbled bread, and season with mace and pepper ; cover them with crumbs of bread and bits of butter; put in the rest of the oysters, season and cover them in the same way. Strain their liquor. and pour over. If you fear they will be too salt, put fresh water instead. Bake fifteen or twenty minutes.

FRIED OYSTERS.—After they are prepared from the shell, they are dipped in batter, made of eggs and crumbs, seasoned with nutmeg, mace and salt, stirred up well. Fried in lard till brown

VEGETABLE OYSTER.—This vegetable is something like a parsnip; is planted about the same time, ripens about the same time, and requires about the same cooking. It is said to taste very much like real oysters. It is cut in pieces, after being boiled, dipped in batter, and fried in the same way. It is excellent mixed with minced salt fish.

PARTRIDGES should be roasted ten or fifteen minutes longer than chickens, that is, provided they are thick-breasted and plump. Being naturally dry, they should be plentifully basted with butter.

EXTRACTS FROM THE *ENGLISH* FRUGAL HOUSEWIFE.

[It was the intention of the author of the *American* Frugal Housewife, to have given an Appendix from the *English* Frugal Housewife; but upon examination, she found the book so little fitted to the wants of this country, that she has been able to extract but little.]

CHEESE is to be chosen by its moist, smooth coat; if old cheese be rough-coated, ragged, or dry at top, beware of worms. If it be over-full of holes, moist and spongy, it is subject to maggots. If soft or perished places appear, try how deep they go, for the worst part may be hidden.

EGGS.—To prove whether they are good or bad, hold the large end of the egg to your tongue; if it feels warm, it is new; but if cold, it is bad. In proportion to the heat or cold, is the goodness of the egg. Another way to know is to put the egg in a pan of cold water; the fresher the egg, the sooner it will fall to the bottom; if rotten, it will swim. If you keep your eggs in ashes, salt or bran, put the small end downwards; if you turn them endways once a week, they will keep some months.

VEAL.—If the vein in the shoulder look blue or bright red, it is newly killed; but if black, green, or yellow, it is stale. The leg is known to be new by the stiffness of the joint. The head of a calf or a lamb is known by the eyes; if sunk or wrinkled, it is stale; if plump and lively, it is fresh.

MUTTON.—If it be young, the flesh will pinch tender; if old, it will wrinkle and remain so. If young, the fat will easily part from the lean; if old, it will stick by strings and skins. Strong, rancid mutton feels spongy, and does not rise again easily, when dented. The flesh of ewe mutton is paler, of a closer grain, and parts more easily.

BEEF.—Good beef has an open grain, and a tender, oily smooth-
ness; a pleasant carnation color, and clear white suet, betoken
good meat; yellow suet is not so good.

PORK.—If young, the lean will break in pinching, and if you nip
the skin with your nails, it will make a dent; the fat will be soft
and pulpy, like lard. If the lean be tough, and the fat flabby and
spongy, feeling rough, it is old, especially if the rind be stub-
born, and you cannot nip it with your nails. Little kernels, like
nail-shot, in the fat, are a sign that it is measly, and dangerous to
be eaten.

To judge of the age of POULTRY, see page 53.

CARVING.

[Written for the *American* Frugal Housewife.]

To CARVE A TURKEY.—Fix the fork firmly on one side of the
thin bone that rises in the centre of the breast; the fork should be
placed *parallel* with the bone, and as close to it as possible. Cut
the meat from the breast lengthwise, in slices of about half an
inch in thickness. Then turn the turkey upon the side nearest
you, and cut off the leg and the wing; when the knife is passed
between the limbs and the body, and pressed outward, the joint
will be easily perceived. Then turn the turkey on the other side,
and cut off the other leg and wing. Separate the drum-sticks
from the leg-bones, and the pinions from the wings; it is hardly
possible to mistake the joint. Cut the stuffing in thin slices,
lengthwise. Take off the neck-bones, which are two triangular
bones on each side of the breast; this is done by passing the
knife from the back under the blade-part of each neck-bone, until
it reaches the end; by raising the knife, the other branch will
easily crack off. Separate the carcass from the back by passing
the knife lengthwise from the neck downward. Turn the back
upwards, and lay the edge of the knife across the back-bone,
about midway between the legs and wings; at the same moment,
place the fork within the lower part of the turkey, and lift it up;
this will make the back-bone crack at the knife. The croup, or
lower part of the back, being cut off, put it on the plate, with the
rump from you, and split off the side-bones by forcing the knife
through from the rump to the other end.
The choicest parts of a turkey are the side-bones, the breast,

and the thigh-bones. The breast and wings are called light meat; the thigh-bones and side-bones dark meat. When a person declines expressing a preference, it is polite to help to both kinds.

A SIRLOIN OF BEEF.—Place the curving bone downward upon the dish. Cut the outside lengthwise, separating *each slice* from the chine-bone, with the point of the knife. Some people cut through at the chine, slip the knife under, and cut the meat out in one mass, which they afterward cut in slices; but this is not the best, or the most proper way. The tender loin is on the inside; it is to be cut crosswise.

A HAM.—Begin in the middle of a ham; cut across the bone, and take thin slices from either side.

A GOOSE.—A goose is carved nearly as a turkey, only the breast should be cut in slices narrow and nearly square, instead of broad, like that of turkey; and before passing the knife to separate the legs and wings, the fork is to be placed in the small end of the leg-bone or pinion, and the part pressed close to the body, when the separation will be easy. Take off the merrythought, the neck-bones, and separate the leg-bones from the legs, and the pinions from the wings. The best parts are the breast, the thigh-bones, and the fleshy parts of the wings.

A PIG.—If the pig be whole, cut off the head, and split it in halves along the back-bone. Separate the shoulders and legs by passing the knife under them in a circular direction. The best parts are the triangular piece of the neck, the ribs, legs and shoulders.

A FILLET OF VEAL.—This is the thick part of the leg, and is to be cut smooth, round and close to the bone. Some prefer the outside piece. A little fat cut from the skirt is to be served to each plate.

MUTTON.—A saddle of mutton is the two loins together, and the back-bone running down the middle to the tail. Slices are to be cut out parallel to the back-bone on either side.

In a leg of mutton, the knife is to be entered in the thick fleshy part, as near the shank as will give a good slice. Cut towards the large end, and always to the bone.

INDEX.

———

	Page
Advice, General,	3 to 8
Alamode Beef,	49
Apple Pie,	67
Apple Pudding,	63
Apple Water,	32
Arrow-root Jelly,	31
Ashes, Care of,	16
Ashes for Land,	13
Asparagus,	34
Balm of Gilead,	26
Batter Pudding,	61
Beans and Peas, cooked,	51
Bed-bug Poison,	10
Beef, cooked,	48
Beef, corned,	40
Beef, salted,	40
Beef Soup,	48
Beef Tea,	32
Beer,	86
Bees, Sting of,	29
Bird's Nest Pudding,	63
Bleeding Wounds,	26
Blisters of Burns broken,	29
Bottles of Rose-water,	14
Bottles, Vials, &c.,	14
Brass Andirons, &c.,	11
Brass Kettles,	11
Brasses in Summer,	16
Bread, Yeast, &c.,	76 to 80
Bread Pudding,	62
Brine,	40, 41, 42
Britannia Ware,	10
Brooms,	17
Broth,	49
Bruises,	36
Buffalo's Tongue,	43
Burdock Leaves,	37
Burns,	28
Butter,	15
Cabbages,	34
Cakes,	70 to 76
Calf's-foot Jelly,	31
Calf's Head,	47
Cancers,	26
Canker,	28

Carpets, ... 11
Carrot Pie, ... 67
Castor Oil, boiled, ... 29
Catsup, ... 35
Celery, ... 35
Cement, ... 19
Cheapest Pieces of Meat, ... 43 to 46
Cheeses, ... 14, 86
Cherry Pie, ... 67
Cherry Pudding, ... 63
Chickens, ... 53
Chicken Broth 55
Chicken fricasseed, ... 54
Chicken Pie, ... 56
Chilblains, ... 27
Chocolate, ... 83
Cholera Morbus, ... 25, 29
Chopped Hands, ... 27
Chowder, ... 59
Cider Cake, ... 71
Clams, ... 58
Clothes Line, &c, ... 17
Clothes washed, ... 17
Cockroaches, ... 19
Cod, ... 57
Coffee, ... 82
Colds, ... 27, 36
Coloring, ... 38 to 40
Combs, ... 9, 20
Cooling Ointments, ... 29, 26
Corn, ... 34
Coughs, ... 36, 37
Court Plaster, ... 20
Cranberry Pie, ... 68
Cranberry Pudding, ... 64
Croup, or Quincy, ... 24
Cucumbers, ... 18
Cucumbers, pickled, ... 85
Cup Cake, ... 71
Currant Jelly, ... 81
Currant-leaf Tea, ... 13
Currant Wine, ... 82
Curry Fowl, ... 54
Custards, cheap, ... 65
Custard Pie, ... 68
Custard Pudding, ... 62
Cut Wounds, ... 25

Dandelions, ... 34
Diet Bread, ... 71
Dish-water, ... 16
Dough Nuts, ... 73
Ducks, ... 55
Dye Stuffs, ... 38 to 40
Dysentery, ... 25, 29, 37

Dyspepsia, ... 24, 37, 65
Dyspepsia Bread, ... 78

Ear-ache, ... 24
Earthen Ware, ... 11
Education of Daughters, ... 91
Eggs, ... 11
Egg Gruel, ... 31
Election Cake, ... 71
Elixir Proprietatis, ... 28

Faded Carpets, Cloth, &c, ... 9
Feathers, and Feather Beds, ... 12
Fevers, ... 28, 37
Fish, fried, ... 58
Fish, salt, ... 59, 60
Flour Pudding, ... 61
Fresh Meat in Summer, ... 17, 47
Fresh Wounds, ... 27
Fried Pork and Apples, ... 60
Fritters, or Flatjacks, ... 74
Furniture, ... 89

Geese, ... 55
Gingerbread, ... 70
Ginger Beer, ... 86
Glass, cut, ... 20
Glass Stoppers, ... 20
Gloves, white, ... 10, 18
Gold cleansed, ... 21
Gravy for Fish, ... 58
Gravy for Meat, ... 52
Gravy for Poultry, ... 57
Green Peas, ... 34
Gruel, ... 30

Haddock, ... 57, 58
Hair, ... 12
Hams, cured, ... 41, 42
Hasty Pudding, ... 65
Head-ache, ... 26, 36
Hearths, ... 18
Herbs, ... 36 to 37
Honey, ... 22
Horseradish, ... 18
Horseradish Leaves, ... 18
How to endure Poverty, ... 111

Icing for Cake, ... 72
Indian Cakes, ... 75, 76
Indian Puddings, ... 61
Inflamed Wounds, ... 29
Inflammation, ... 24
Iron, ... 11
Ironing, ... 17

Jaundice, ... 28

Knife Handles, ... 9
Knives, washed, ... 14

Lamb, cooked, ... 49
Lard, ... 14, 15
Leaven, ... 80
Lemon Brandy, ... 18
Lemon Syrup, ... 20
Lettuce, ... 85
Loaf Cake, ... 72
Lobster, ... 60
Lockjaw, ... 24

Mackerel, ... 58, 59, 60
Mangoes, ... 84
Marble Fireplaces, ... 12
Martinoes, ... 85
Mats for the Table, ... 10
Mattresses, ... 15
Maxims for Health, ... 87 to 88
Meal, ... 9
Meat, Choice of, ... 43 to 46
Meat, corned and salted, ... 40 to 43
Meat Pie, ... 56
Meat in Summer, ... 17, 47
Milk Porridge, ... 82
Mince Meat, ... 50
Mince Pies, ... 66
Molasses, ... 16, 29
Mortification, ... 27
Moths, ... 13
Mutton, corned and dried, ... 41
Mutton and Lamb, cooked, ... 49

Nasturtion-seed, pickled, ... 85
Navarino Bonnets, ... 13
Nerves, excited, ... 37
Night Sweats, ... 29

Ointment of Elder Buds, ... 29
Ointment of Ground Worms, ... 26
Ointment of House Leek, ... 26
Ointment of Lard, ... 29
Ointment of Lard and Sulphur, ... 28
Oil, sweet, ... 18
Old Clothes, ... 13
Onions, ... 33, 36
Ovens, heated, ... 78

Pancakes, ... 74
Paper, ... 15
Parsnips, ... 84
Pastry, ... 69

Peas, dry, ... 51
Peas, green, ... 84
Philosophy and Consistency, ... 104
Pickles, ... 84, 85
Pictures, covered, ... 17
Pie Crust, ... 69
Pig, roasted, ... 50
Pigeons, ... 56
Piles, ... 28, 37
Plum Puddings, ... 64
Potatoes, ... 34
Potato Cheese, ... 86
Pork, cooked, ... 49
Pork, salted, ... 40
Poultry, injured, ... 57
Poultry, young or old, ... 58
Preserves, ... 81
Provisions, ... 17
Prunes, stewed, ... 33
Puddings, ... 61 to 65
Pump Handle, ... 16
Pumpkin Pie, ... 66

Rags, ... 12, 16
Raspberry Shrub, ... 82
Rattlesnake-bite, ... 30
Reasons for Hard Times, ... 108
Red Ants, ... 21
Rennet Pudding, ... 62
Rhubarb or Persian Apple Pie, ... 69
Rice Bread, ... 78
Rice Pudding, ... 63
Ring-worms, ... 30
Run Rounds, ... 30
Rusty Crape, ... 11
Rusty Silk, ... 19
Rye Paste, ... 21

Sago Jelly, ... 32
Salt Fish, ... 59
Salt Fish, warmed, ... 60
Sauces for Pudding, ... 65
Sausages, ... 50
Short Cake, ... 75
Silk, washed, ... 14
Sinews, contracted, ... 26
Soap, ... 22, 23
Soda Powders, ... 20
Sore Mouth, ... 28
Sore Throat, ... 26
Soup, ... 48
Souse, ... 52
Sponge Cake, ... 71
Spots on Furniture, Cloth, &c. 10
Sprain, ... 24

Squashes, ... 34, 35
Squash Pie, ... 66
Starch, ... 19
Stewed Prunes, ... 33
Sting of Bees,* 29
Stockings, ... 19
Straw Beds, ... 16
Straw Carpets, ... 21
Suet, ... 15
Sweet Marjoram, ... 37
Swellings, ... 27

Tapioca Jelly, ... 31
Tea, ... 84
Tea Cake, ... 71
Teeth, ... 12
Throat Distemper, ... 27
Toe Nails, ... 30
Tomatoes, ... 35
Tongue, ... 42, 43
Tooth-ache, ... 29
Tortoise-shell Combs, ... 20
Towels, ... 17
Travelling and Public Amusements, ... 99
Tripe, ... 52
Turkeys, ... 55

Vapor Bath, ... 27
Veal, cooked, ... 47
Vegetables, ... 33 to 36
Vials, ... 17
Vinegar, ... 15

Walnuts, pickled, ... 84
Wash-leather Gloves, ... 11
Water, purified, ... 14
Water, soft, ... 13
Wax, ... 22
Wedding Cake, ... 72
Wens, ... 27
White Kid Gloves, ... 10, 13
Whortleberry Pie, ... 67
Whortleberry Pudding, ... 64
Wicks of Lamps, Candles, &c. 10
Wine Whey, ... 32
Woollens, washed, ... 14
Woollen Yarn, ... 11
Worms, ... 24

Yeast, ... 79, 80

APPENDIX.

Apple Marmalade, ... 118

Beef, ... 122
Blanc Manger, ... 118
Brass Kettles, ... 115
Bread without yeast, ... 117
Bruises, ... 116
Burns, ... 116
Butter, tainted, ... 114

Cancers, ... 116
Candles, ... 114
Carving, Directions for, 122, 123
Cheese, ... 121
Chloride of Lime, ... 117
Cocoa-nut Cakes, ... 119
Cologne Water, ... 117
Corns, ... 117
Cranberry Jelly, ... 119
Cream 114
Currants, green, preserved, 114
Custards, rich, ... 119

Ear-Wax, ... 116
Eggs, ... 121
Eggs in winter, ... 117

Feathers, ... 115
Flowers, ... 115
Frosting for Cake, ... 120
Furniture, ... 114

Grease Spots, ... 117

Heart-Burn 117
Horse-Flies, ... 115

Icy Steps, ... 115

Ink Spots, ... 115

Lobster Salad, ... 120

Mutton, ... 121

Oysters escaloped and fried, 120
Oysters, Vegetable, ... 121

Partridges, ... 121
Peaches, preserved, ... 119
Pearls, ... 117
Piles, ... 116
Pine Apples, ... 115
Pork, ... 122
Pork Jelly, ... 119
Pumpkin Pies, ... 115
Pumpkin, dried, ... 115

Quince Marmalade, ... 118

Raspberry Jam, ... 118
Rice Jelly, ... 118

Sore Nipples, ... 116
Starch, ... 115
Sugar, clarified, ... 20, 119

Teeth, ... 114
Tomatoes Pie, ... 114

Varnishing Gilded Frames, 117
Veal, ... 121

Warts, ... 116
Wasp-Sting, ... 116
Wedding Cake, rich, ...119, 120
Whips, ... 120
White-washing, ... 115

A CATALOG OF SELECTED
DOVER BOOKS
IN ALL FIELDS OF INTEREST

A CATALOG OF SELECTED DOVER
BOOKS IN ALL FIELDS OF INTEREST

100 BEST-LOVED POEMS, Edited by Philip Smith. "The Passionate Shepherd to His Love," "Shall I compare thee to a summer's day?" "Death, be not proud," "The Raven," "The Road Not Taken," plus works by Blake, Wordsworth, Byron, Shelley, Keats, many others. 96pp. 5³⁄₁₆ x 8¼.   0-486-28553-7

100 SMALL HOUSES OF THE THIRTIES, Brown-Blodgett Company. Exterior photographs and floor plans for 100 charming structures. Illustrations of models accompanied by descriptions of interiors, color schemes, closet space, and other amenities. 200 illustrations. 112pp. 8⅜ x 11.   0-486-44131-8

1000 TURN-OF-THE-CENTURY HOUSES: With Illustrations and Floor Plans, Herbert C. Chivers. Reproduced from a rare edition, this showcase of homes ranges from cottages and bungalows to sprawling mansions. Each house is meticulously illustrated and accompanied by complete floor plans. 256pp. 9⅜ x 12¼.

                                                    0-486-45596-3

101 GREAT AMERICAN POEMS, Edited by The American Poetry & Literacy Project. Rich treasury of verse from the 19th and 20th centuries includes works by Edgar Allan Poe, Robert Frost, Walt Whitman, Langston Hughes, Emily Dickinson, T. S. Eliot, other notables. 96pp. 5³⁄₁₆ x 8¼.   0-486-40158-8

101 GREAT SAMURAI PRINTS, Utagawa Kuniyoshi. Kuniyoshi was a master of the warrior woodblock print — and these 18th-century illustrations represent the pinnacle of his craft. Full-color portraits of renowned Japanese samurais pulse with movement, passion, and remarkably fine detail. 112pp. 8⅜ x 11.   0-486-46523-3

ABC OF BALLET, Janet Grosser. Clearly worded, abundantly illustrated little guide defines basic ballet-related terms: arabesque, battement, pas de chat, relevé, sissonne, many others. Pronunciation guide included. Excellent primer. 48pp. 4³⁄₁₆ x 5¾.

                                                      0-486-40871-X

ACCESSORIES OF DRESS: An Illustrated Encyclopedia, Katherine Lester and Bess Viola Oerke. Illustrations of hats, veils, wigs, cravats, shawls, shoes, gloves, and other accessories enhance an engaging commentary that reveals the humor and charm of the many-sided story of accessorized apparel. 644 figures and 59 plates. 608pp. 6⅛ x 9¼.

                                                      0-486-43378-1

ADVENTURES OF HUCKLEBERRY FINN, Mark Twain. Join Huck and Jim as their boyhood adventures along the Mississippi River lead them into a world of excitement, danger, and self-discovery. Humorous narrative, lyrical descriptions of the Mississippi valley, and memorable characters. 224pp. 5³⁄₁₆ x 8¼.   0-486-28061-6

ALICE STARMORE'S BOOK OF FAIR ISLE KNITTING, Alice Starmore. A noted designer from the region of Scotland's Fair Isle explores the history and techniques of this distinctive, stranded-color knitting style and provides copious illustrated instructions for 14 original knitwear designs. 208pp. 8⅜ x 10⅞.   0-486-47218-3

Browse over 9,000 books at www.doverpublications.com

ALICE'S ADVENTURES IN WONDERLAND, Lewis Carroll. Beloved classic about a little girl lost in a topsy-turvy land and her encounters with the White Rabbit, March Hare, Mad Hatter, Cheshire Cat, and other delightfully improbable characters. 42 illustrations by Sir John Tenniel. 96pp. 5³⁄₁₆ x 8¼. 0-486-27543-4

AMERICA'S LIGHTHOUSES: An Illustrated History, Francis Ross Holland. Profusely illustrated fact-filled survey of American lighthouses since 1716. Over 200 stations — East, Gulf, and West coasts, Great Lakes, Hawaii, Alaska, Puerto Rico, the Virgin Islands, and the Mississippi and St. Lawrence Rivers. 240pp. 8 x 10¾. 0-486-25576-X

AN ENCYCLOPEDIA OF THE VIOLIN, Alberto Bachmann. Translated by Frederick H. Martens. Introduction by Eugene Ysaye. First published in 1925, this renowned reference remains unsurpassed as a source of essential information, from construction and evolution to repertoire and technique. Includes a glossary and 73 illustrations. 496pp. 6⅛ x 9¼. 0-486-46618-3

ANIMALS: 1,419 Copyright-Free Illustrations of Mammals, Birds, Fish, Insects, etc., Selected by Jim Harter. Selected for its visual impact and ease of use, this outstanding collection of wood engravings presents over 1,000 species of animals in extremely lifelike poses. Includes mammals, birds, reptiles, amphibians, fish, insects, and other invertebrates. 284pp. 9 x 12. 0-486-23766-4

THE ANNALS, Tacitus. Translated by Alfred John Church and William Jackson Brodribb. This vital chronicle of Imperial Rome, written by the era's great historian, spans A.D. 14-68 and paints incisive psychological portraits of major figures, from Tiberius to Nero. 416pp. 5³⁄₁₆ x 8¼. 0-486-45236-0

ANTIGONE, Sophocles. Filled with passionate speeches and sensitive probing of moral and philosophical issues, this powerful and often-performed Greek drama reveals the grim fate that befalls the children of Oedipus. Footnotes. 64pp. 5³⁄₁₆ x 8 ¼. 0-486-27804-2

ART DECO DECORATIVE PATTERNS IN FULL COLOR, Christian Stoll. Reprinted from a rare 1910 portfolio, 160 sensuous and exotic images depict a breathtaking array of florals, geometrics, and abstracts — all elegant in their stark simplicity. 64pp. 8⅜ x 11. 0-486-44862-2

THE ARTHUR RACKHAM TREASURY: 86 Full-Color Illustrations, Arthur Rackham. Selected and Edited by Jeff A. Menges. A stunning treasury of 86 full-page plates span the famed English artist's career, from *Rip Van Winkle* (1905) to masterworks such as *Undine*, *A Midsummer Night's Dream*, and *Wind in the Willows* (1939). 96pp. 8⅜ x 11. 0-486-44685-9

THE AUTHENTIC GILBERT & SULLIVAN SONGBOOK, W. S. Gilbert and A. S. Sullivan. The most comprehensive collection available, this songbook includes selections from every one of Gilbert and Sullivan's light operas. Ninety-two numbers are presented uncut and unedited, and in their original keys. 410pp. 9 x 12. 0-486-23482-7

THE AWAKENING, Kate Chopin. First published in 1899, this controversial novel of a New Orleans wife's search for love outside a stifling marriage shocked readers. Today, it remains a first-rate narrative with superb characterization. New introductory Note. 128pp. 5³⁄₁₆ x 8¼. 0-486-27786-0

BASIC DRAWING, Louis Priscilla. Beginning with perspective, this commonsense manual progresses to the figure in movement, light and shade, anatomy, drapery, composition, trees and landscape, and outdoor sketching. Black-and-white illustrations throughout. 128pp. 8⅜ x 11. 0-486-45815-6

Browse over 9,000 books at www.doverpublications.com

THE BATTLES THAT CHANGED HISTORY, Fletcher Pratt. Historian profiles 16 crucial conflicts, ancient to modern, that changed the course of Western civilization. Gripping accounts of battles led by Alexander the Great, Joan of Arc, Ulysses S. Grant, other commanders. 27 maps. 352pp. 5⅜ x 8½. 0-486-41129-X

BEETHOVEN'S LETTERS, Ludwig van Beethoven. Edited by Dr. A. C. Kalischer. Features 457 letters to fellow musicians, friends, greats, patrons, and literary men. Reveals musical thoughts, quirks of personality, insights, and daily events. Includes 15 plates. 410pp. 5⅜ x 8½. 0-486-22769-3

BERNICE BOBS HER HAIR AND OTHER STORIES, F. Scott Fitzgerald. This brilliant anthology includes 6 of Fitzgerald's most popular stories: "The Diamond as Big as the Ritz," the title tale, "The Offshore Pirate," "The Ice Palace," "The Jelly Bean," and "May Day." 176pp. 5⅜ x 8½. 0-486-47049-0

BESLER'S BOOK OF FLOWERS AND PLANTS: 73 Full-Color Plates from Hortus Eystettensis, 1613, Basilius Besler. Here is a selection of magnificent plates from the *Hortus Eystettensis*, which vividly illustrated and identified the plants, flowers, and trees that thrived in the legendary German garden at Eichstätt. 80pp. 8⅜ x 11. 0-486-46005-3

THE BOOK OF KELLS, Edited by Blanche Cirker. Painstakingly reproduced from a rare facsimile edition, this volume contains full-page decorations, portraits, illustrations, plus a sampling of textual leaves with exquisite calligraphy and ornamentation. 32 full-color illustrations. 32pp. 9⅜ x 12¼. 0-486-24345-1

THE BOOK OF THE CROSSBOW: With an Additional Section on Catapults and Other Siege Engines, Ralph Payne-Gallwey. Fascinating study traces history and use of crossbow as military and sporting weapon, from Middle Ages to modern times. Also covers related weapons: balistas, catapults, Turkish bows, more. Over 240 illustrations. 400pp. 7¼ x 10⅛. 0-486-28720-3

THE BUNGALOW BOOK: Floor Plans and Photos of 112 Houses, 1910, Henry L. Wilson. Here are 112 of the most popular and economic blueprints of the early 20th century — plus an illustration or photograph of each completed house. A wonderful time capsule that still offers a wealth of valuable insights. 160pp. 8⅜ x 11. 0-486-45104-6

THE CALL OF THE WILD, Jack London. A classic novel of adventure, drawn from London's own experiences as a Klondike adventurer, relating the story of a heroic dog caught in the brutal life of the Alaska Gold Rush. Note. 64pp. 5³⁄₁₆ x 8¼. 0-486-26472-6

CANDIDE, Voltaire. Edited by Francois-Marie Arouet. One of the world's great satires since its first publication in 1759. Witty, caustic skewering of romance, science, philosophy, religion, government — nearly all human ideals and institutions. 112pp. 5³⁄₁₆ x 8¼. 0-486-26689-3

CELEBRATED IN THEIR TIME: Photographic Portraits from the George Grantham Bain Collection, Edited by Amy Pastan. With an Introduction by Michael Carlebach. Remarkable portrait gallery features 112 rare images of Albert Einstein, Charlie Chaplin, the Wright Brothers, Henry Ford, and other luminaries from the worlds of politics, art, entertainment, and industry. 128pp. 8⅜ x 11. 0-486-46754-6

CHARIOTS FOR APOLLO: The NASA History of Manned Lunar Spacecraft to 1969, Courtney G. Brooks, James M. Grimwood, and Loyd S. Swenson, Jr. This illustrated history by a trio of experts is the definitive reference on the Apollo spacecraft and lunar modules. It traces the vehicles' design, development, and operation in space. More than 100 photographs and illustrations. 576pp. 6¾ x 9¼. 0-486-46756-2

Browse over 9,000 books at www.doverpublications.com

A CHRISTMAS CAROL, Charles Dickens. This engrossing tale relates Ebenezer Scrooge's ghostly journeys through Christmases past, present, and future and his ultimate transformation from a harsh and grasping old miser to a charitable and compassionate human being. 80pp. 5³⁄₁₆ x 8¼. 0-486-26865-9

COMMON SENSE, Thomas Paine. First published in January of 1776, this highly influential landmark document clearly and persuasively argued for American separation from Great Britain and paved the way for the Declaration of Independence. 64pp. 5³⁄₁₆ x 8¼. 0-486-29602-4

THE COMPLETE SHORT STORIES OF OSCAR WILDE, Oscar Wilde. Complete texts of "The Happy Prince and Other Tales," "A House of Pomegranates," "Lord Arthur Savile's Crime and Other Stories," "Poems in Prose," and "The Portrait of Mr. W. H." 208pp. 5³⁄₁₆ x 8¼. 0-486-45216-6

COMPLETE SONNETS, William Shakespeare. Over 150 exquisite poems deal with love, friendship, the tyranny of time, beauty's evanescence, death, and other themes in language of remarkable power, precision, and beauty. Glossary of archaic terms. 80pp. 5³⁄₁₆ x 8¼. 0-486-26686-9

THE COUNT OF MONTE CRISTO: Abridged Edition, Alexandre Dumas. Falsely accused of treason, Edmond Dantès is imprisoned in the bleak Chateau d'If. After a hair-raising escape, he launches an elaborate plot to extract a bitter revenge against those who betrayed him. 448pp. 5³⁄₁₆ x 8¼. 0-486-45643-9

CRAFTSMAN BUNGALOWS: Designs from the Pacific Northwest, Yoho & Merritt. This reprint of a rare catalog, showcasing the charming simplicity and cozy style of Craftsman bungalows, is filled with photos of completed homes, plus floor plans and estimated costs. An indispensable resource for architects, historians, and illustrators. 112pp. 10 x 7. 0-486-46875-5

CRAFTSMAN BUNGALOWS: 59 Homes from "The Craftsman," Edited by Gustav Stickley. Best and most attractive designs from Arts and Crafts Movement publication — 1903–1916 — includes sketches, photographs of homes, floor plans, descriptive text. 128pp. 8¼ x 11. 0-486-25829-7

CRIME AND PUNISHMENT, Fyodor Dostoyevsky. Translated by Constance Garnett. Supreme masterpiece tells the story of Raskolnikov, a student tormented by his own thoughts after he murders an old woman. Overwhelmed by guilt and terror, he confesses and goes to prison. 480pp. 5³⁄₁₆ x 8¼. 0-486-41587-2

THE DECLARATION OF INDEPENDENCE AND OTHER GREAT DOCUMENTS OF AMERICAN HISTORY: 1775-1865, Edited by John Grafton. Thirteen compelling and influential documents: Henry's "Give Me Liberty or Give Me Death," Declaration of Independence, The Constitution, Washington's First Inaugural Address, The Monroe Doctrine, The Emancipation Proclamation, Gettysburg Address, more. 64pp. 5³⁄₁₆ x 8¼. 0-486-41124-9

THE DESERT AND THE SOWN: Travels in Palestine and Syria, Gertrude Bell. "The female Lawrence of Arabia," Gertrude Bell wrote captivating, perceptive accounts of her travels in the Middle East. This intriguing narrative, accompanied by 160 photos, traces her 1905 sojourn in Lebanon, Syria, and Palestine. 368pp. 5⅜ x 8½. 0-486-46876-3

A DOLL'S HOUSE, Henrik Ibsen. Ibsen's best-known play displays his genius for realistic prose drama. An expression of women's rights, the play climaxes when the central character, Nora, rejects a smothering marriage and life in "a doll's house." 80pp. 5³⁄₁₆ x 8¼. 0-486-27062-9

Browse over 9,000 books at www.doverpublications.com

DOOMED SHIPS: Great Ocean Liner Disasters, William H. Miller, Jr. Nearly 200 photographs, many from private collections, highlight tales of some of the vessels whose pleasure cruises ended in catastrophe: the *Morro Castle, Normandie, Andrea Doria, Europa,* and many others. 128pp. 8⅜ x 11¼. 0-486-45366-9

THE DORÉ BIBLE ILLUSTRATIONS, Gustave Doré. Detailed plates from the Bible: the Creation scenes, Adam and Eve, horrifying visions of the Flood, the battle sequences with their monumental crowds, depictions of the life of Jesus, 241 plates in all. 241pp. 9 x 12. 0-486-23004-X

DRAWING DRAPERY FROM HEAD TO TOE, Cliff Young. Expert guidance on how to draw shirts, pants, skirts, gloves, hats, and coats on the human figure, including folds in relation to the body, pull and crush, action folds, creases, more. Over 200 drawings. 48pp. 8¼ x 11. 0-486-45591-2

DUBLINERS, James Joyce. A fine and accessible introduction to the work of one of the 20th century's most influential writers, this collection features 15 tales, including a masterpiece of the short-story genre, "The Dead." 160pp. 5³⁄₁₆ x 8¼. 0-486-26870-5

EASY-TO-MAKE POP-UPS, Joan Irvine. Illustrated by Barbara Reid. Dozens of wonderful ideas for three-dimensional paper fun — from holiday greeting cards with moving parts to a pop-up menagerie. Easy-to-follow, illustrated instructions for more than 30 projects. 299 black-and-white illustrations. 96pp. 8⅜ x 11. 0-486-44622-0

EASY-TO-MAKE STORYBOOK DOLLS: A "Novel" Approach to Cloth Dollmaking, Sherralyn St. Clair. Favorite fictional characters come alive in this unique beginner's dollmaking guide. Includes patterns for Pollyanna, Dorothy from *The Wonderful Wizard of Oz*, Mary of *The Secret Garden*, plus easy-to-follow instructions, 263 black-and-white illustrations, and an 8-page color insert. 112pp. 8¼ x 11. 0-486-47360-0

EINSTEIN'S ESSAYS IN SCIENCE, Albert Einstein. Speeches and essays in accessible, everyday language profile influential physicists such as Niels Bohr and Isaac Newton. They also explore areas of physics to which the author made major contributions. 128pp. 5 x 8. 0-486-47011-3

EL DORADO: Further Adventures of the Scarlet Pimpernel, Baroness Orczy. A popular sequel to *The Scarlet Pimpernel*, this suspenseful story recounts the Pimpernel's attempts to rescue the Dauphin from imprisonment during the French Revolution. An irresistible blend of intrigue, period detail, and vibrant characterizations. 352pp. 5³⁄₁₆ x 8¼. 0-486-44026-5

ELEGANT SMALL HOMES OF THE TWENTIES: 99 Designs from a Competition, Chicago Tribune. Nearly 100 designs for five- and six-room houses feature New England and Southern colonials, Normandy cottages, stately Italianate dwellings, and other fascinating snapshots of American domestic architecture of the 1920s. 112pp. 9 x 12. 0-486-46910-7

THE ELEMENTS OF STYLE: The Original Edition, William Strunk, Jr. This is the book that generations of writers have relied upon for timeless advice on grammar, diction, syntax, and other essentials. In concise terms, it identifies the principal requirements of proper style and common errors. 64pp. 5⅜ x 8½. 0-486-44798-7

THE ELUSIVE PIMPERNEL, Baroness Orczy. Robespierre's revolutionaries find their wicked schemes thwarted by the heroic Pimpernel — Sir Percival Blakeney. In this thrilling sequel, Chauvelin devises a plot to eliminate the Pimpernel and his wife. 272pp. 5³⁄₁₆ x 8¼. 0-486-45464-9

AN ENCYCLOPEDIA OF BATTLES: Accounts of Over 1,560 Battles from 1479 B.C. to the Present, David Eggenberger. Essential details of every major battle in recorded history from the first battle of Megiddo in 1479 B.C. to Grenada in 1984. List of battle maps. 99 illustrations. 544pp. 6½ x 9¼. 0-486-24913-1

ENCYCLOPEDIA OF EMBROIDERY STITCHES, INCLUDING CREWEL, Marion Nichols. Precise explanations and instructions, clearly illustrated, on how to work chain, back, cross, knotted, woven stitches, and many more — 178 in all, including Cable Outline, Whipped Satin, and Eyelet Buttonhole. Over 1400 illustrations. 219pp. 8⅜ x 11¼. 0-486-22929-7

ENTER JEEVES: 15 Early Stories, P. G. Wodehouse. Splendid collection contains first 8 stories featuring Bertie Wooster, the deliciously dim aristocrat and Jeeves, his brainy, imperturbable manservant. Also, the complete Reggie Pepper (Bertie's prototype) series. 288pp. 5⅜ x 8½. 0-486-29717-9

ERIC SLOANE'S AMERICA: Paintings in Oil, Michael Wigley. With a Foreword by Mimi Sloane. Eric Sloane's evocative oils of America's landscape and material culture shimmer with immense historical and nostalgic appeal. This original hardcover collection gathers nearly a hundred of his finest paintings, with subjects ranging from New England to the American Southwest. 128pp. 10⅝ x 9. 0-486-46525-X

ETHAN FROME, Edith Wharton. Classic story of wasted lives, set against a bleak New England background. Superbly delineated characters in a hauntingly grim tale of thwarted love. Considered by many to be Wharton's masterpiece. 96pp. 5³⁄₁₆ x 8 ¼. 0-486-26690-7

THE EVERLASTING MAN, G. K. Chesterton. Chesterton's view of Christianity — as a blend of philosophy and mythology, satisfying intellect and spirit — applies to his brilliant book, which appeals to readers' heads as well as their hearts. 288pp. 5⅜ x 8½. 0-486-46036-3

THE FIELD AND FOREST HANDY BOOK, Daniel Beard. Written by a co-founder of the Boy Scouts, this appealing guide offers illustrated instructions for building kites, birdhouses, boats, igloos, and other fun projects, plus numerous helpful tips for campers. 448pp. 5³⁄₁₆ x 8¼. 0-486-46191-2

FINDING YOUR WAY WITHOUT MAP OR COMPASS, Harold Gatty. Useful, instructive manual shows would-be explorers, hikers, bikers, scouts, sailors, and survivalists how to find their way outdoors by observing animals, weather patterns, shifting sands, and other elements of nature. 288pp. 5⅜ x 8½. 0-486-40613-X

FIRST FRENCH READER: A Beginner's Dual-Language Book, Edited and Translated by Stanley Appelbaum. This anthology introduces 50 legendary writers — Voltaire, Balzac, Baudelaire, Proust, more — through passages from *The Red and the Black, Les Misérables, Madame Bovary,* and other classics. Original French text plus English translation on facing pages. 240pp. 5⅜ x 8½. 0-486-46178-5

FIRST GERMAN READER: A Beginner's Dual-Language Book, Edited by Harry Steinhauer. Specially chosen for their power to evoke German life and culture, these short, simple readings include poems, stories, essays, and anecdotes by Goethe, Hesse, Heine, Schiller, and others. 224pp. 5⅜ x 8½. 0-486-46179-3

FIRST SPANISH READER: A Beginner's Dual-Language Book, Angel Flores. Delightful stories, other material based on works of Don Juan Manuel, Luis Taboada, Ricardo Palma, other noted writers. Complete faithful English translations on facing pages. Exercises. 176pp. 5⅜ x 8½. 0-486-25810-6

Browse over 9,000 books at www.doverpublications.com

FIVE ACRES AND INDEPENDENCE, Maurice G. Kains. Great back-to-the-land classic explains basics of self-sufficient farming. The one book to get. 95 illustrations. 397pp. 5⅜ x 8½. 0-486-20974-1

FLAGG'S SMALL HOUSES: Their Economic Design and Construction, 1922, Ernest Flagg. Although most famous for his skyscrapers, Flagg was also a proponent of the well-designed single-family dwelling. His classic treatise features innovations that save space, materials, and cost. 526 illustrations. 160pp. 9⅜ x 12¼. 0-486-45197-6

FLATLAND: A Romance of Many Dimensions, Edwin A. Abbott. Classic of science (and mathematical) fiction — charmingly illustrated by the author — describes the adventures of A. Square, a resident of Flatland, in Spaceland (three dimensions), Lineland (one dimension), and Pointland (no dimensions). 96pp. 5³⁄₁₆ x 8¼. 0-486-27263-X

FRANKENSTEIN, Mary Shelley. The story of Victor Frankenstein's monstrous creation and the havoc it caused has enthralled generations of readers and inspired countless writers of horror and suspense. With the author's own 1831 introduction. 176pp. 5³⁄₁₆ x 8¼. 0-486-28211-2

THE GARGOYLE BOOK: 572 Examples from Gothic Architecture, Lester Burbank Bridaham. Dispelling the conventional wisdom that French Gothic architectural flourishes were born of despair or gloom, Bridaham reveals the whimsical nature of these creations and the ingenious artisans who made them. 572 illustrations. 224pp. 8⅜ x 11. 0-486-44754-5

THE GIFT OF THE MAGI AND OTHER SHORT STORIES, O. Henry. Sixteen captivating stories by one of America's most popular storytellers. Included are such classics as "The Gift of the Magi," "The Last Leaf," and "The Ransom of Red Chief." Publisher's Note. 96pp. 5³⁄₁₆ x 8¼. 0-486-27061-0

THE GOETHE TREASURY: Selected Prose and Poetry, Johann Wolfgang von Goethe. Edited, Selected, and with an Introduction by Thomas Mann. In addition to his lyric poetry, Goethe wrote travel sketches, autobiographical studies, essays, letters, and proverbs in rhyme and prose. This collection presents outstanding examples from each genre. 368pp. 5⅜ x 8½. 0-486-44780-4

GREAT EXPECTATIONS, Charles Dickens. Orphaned Pip is apprenticed to the dirty work of the forge but dreams of becoming a gentleman — and one day finds himself in possession of "great expectations." Dickens' finest novel. 400pp. 5³⁄₁₆ x 8¼. 0-486-41586-4

GREAT WRITERS ON THE ART OF FICTION: From Mark Twain to Joyce Carol Oates, Edited by James Daley. An indispensable source of advice and inspiration, this anthology features essays by Henry James, Kate Chopin, Willa Cather, Sinclair Lewis, Jack London, Raymond Chandler, Raymond Carver, Eudora Welty, and Kurt Vonnegut, Jr. 192pp. 5⅜ x 8½. 0-486-45128-3

HAMLET, William Shakespeare. The quintessential Shakespearean tragedy, whose highly charged confrontations and anguished soliloquies probe depths of human feeling rarely sounded in any art. Reprinted from an authoritative British edition complete with illuminating footnotes. 128pp. 5³⁄₁₆ x 8¼. 0-486-27278-8

THE HAUNTED HOUSE, Charles Dickens. A Yuletide gathering in an eerie country retreat provides the backdrop for Dickens and his friends — including Elizabeth Gaskell and Wilkie Collins — who take turns spinning supernatural yarns. 144pp. 5⅜ x 8½. 0-486-46309-5

HEART OF DARKNESS, Joseph Conrad. Dark allegory of a journey up the Congo River and the narrator's encounter with the mysterious Mr. Kurtz. Masterly blend of adventure, character study, psychological penetration. For many, Conrad's finest, most enigmatic story. 80pp. $5\frac{3}{16} \times 8\frac{1}{4}$. 0-486-26464-5

HENSON AT THE NORTH POLE, Matthew A. Henson. This thrilling memoir by the heroic African-American who was Peary's companion through two decades of Arctic exploration recounts a tale of danger, courage, and determination. "Fascinating and exciting." — *Commonweal.* 128pp. $5\frac{3}{8} \times 8\frac{1}{2}$. 0-486-45472-X

HISTORIC COSTUMES AND HOW TO MAKE THEM, Mary Fernald and E. Shenton. Practical, informative guidebook shows how to create everything from short tunics worn by Saxon men in the fifth century to a lady's bustle dress of the late 1800s. 81 illustrations. 176pp. $5\frac{3}{8} \times 8\frac{1}{2}$. 0-486-44906-8

THE HOUND OF THE BASKERVILLES, Arthur Conan Doyle. A deadly curse in the form of a legendary ferocious beast continues to claim its victims from the Baskerville family until Holmes and Watson intervene. Often called the best detective story ever written. 128pp. $5\frac{3}{16} \times 8\frac{1}{4}$. 0-486-28214-7

THE HOUSE BEHIND THE CEDARS, Charles W. Chesnutt. Originally published in 1900, this groundbreaking novel by a distinguished African-American author recounts the drama of a brother and sister who "pass for white" during the dangerous days of Reconstruction. 208pp. $5\frac{3}{8} \times 8\frac{1}{2}$. 0-486-46144-0

THE HUMAN FIGURE IN MOTION, Eadweard Muybridge. The 4,789 photographs in this definitive selection show the human figure — models almost all undraped — engaged in over 160 different types of action: running, climbing stairs, etc. 390pp. $7\frac{7}{8} \times 10\frac{5}{8}$. 0-486-20204-6

THE IMPORTANCE OF BEING EARNEST, Oscar Wilde. Wilde's witty and buoyant comedy of manners, filled with some of literature's most famous epigrams, reprinted from an authoritative British edition. Considered Wilde's most perfect work. 64pp. $5\frac{3}{16} \times 8\frac{1}{4}$. 0-486-26478-5

THE INFERNO, Dante Alighieri. Translated and with notes by Henry Wadsworth Longfellow. The first stop on Dante's famous journey from Hell to Purgatory to Paradise, this 14th-century allegorical poem blends vivid and shocking imagery with graceful lyricism. Translated by the beloved 19th-century poet, Henry Wadsworth Longfellow. 256pp. $5\frac{3}{16} \times 8\frac{1}{4}$. 0-486-44288-8

JANE EYRE, Charlotte Brontë. Written in 1847, *Jane Eyre* tells the tale of an orphan girl's progress from the custody of cruel relatives to an oppressive boarding school and its culmination in a troubled career as a governess. 448pp. $5\frac{3}{16} \times 8\frac{1}{4}$. 0-486-42449-9

JAPANESE WOODBLOCK FLOWER PRINTS, Tanigami Kônan. Extraordinary collection of Japanese woodblock prints by a well-known artist features 120 plates in brilliant color. Realistic images from a rare edition include daffodils, tulips, and other familiar and unusual flowers. 128pp. $11 \times 8\frac{1}{4}$. 0-486-46442-3

JEWELRY MAKING AND DESIGN, Augustus F. Rose and Antonio Cirino. Professional secrets of jewelry making are revealed in a thorough, practical guide. Over 200 illustrations. 306pp. $5\frac{3}{8} \times 8\frac{1}{2}$. 0-486-21750-7

JULIUS CAESAR, William Shakespeare. Great tragedy based on Plutarch's account of the lives of Brutus, Julius Caesar and Mark Antony. Evil plotting, ringing oratory, high tragedy with Shakespeare's incomparable insight, dramatic power. Explanatory footnotes. 96pp. $5\frac{3}{16} \times 8\frac{1}{4}$. 0-486-26876-4

THE JUNGLE, Upton Sinclair. 1906 bestseller shockingly reveals intolerable labor practices and working conditions in the Chicago stockyards as it tells the grim story of a Slavic family that emigrates to America full of optimism but soon faces despair. 320pp. 5³⁄₁₆ x 8¼. 0-486-41923-1

THE KINGDOM OF GOD IS WITHIN YOU, Leo Tolstoy. The soul-searching book that inspired Gandhi to embrace the concept of passive resistance, Tolstoy's 1894 polemic clearly outlines a radical, well-reasoned revision of traditional Christian thinking. 352pp. 5³⁄₁₆ x 8¼. 0-486-45138-0

THE LADY OR THE TIGER?: and Other Logic Puzzles, Raymond M. Smullyan. Created by a renowned puzzle master, these whimsically themed challenges involve paradoxes about probability, time, and change; metapuzzles; and self-referentiality. Nineteen chapters advance in difficulty from relatively simple to highly complex. 1982 edition. 240pp. 5⅜ x 8½. 0-486-47027-X

LEAVES OF GRASS: The Original 1855 Edition, Walt Whitman. Whitman's immortal collection includes some of the greatest poems of modern times, including his masterpiece, "Song of Myself." Shattering standard conventions, it stands as an unabashed celebration of body and nature. 128pp. 5³⁄₁₆ x 8¼. 0-486-45676-5

LES MISÉRABLES, Victor Hugo. Translated by Charles E. Wilbour. Abridged by James K. Robinson. A convict's heroic struggle for justice and redemption plays out against a fiery backdrop of the Napoleonic wars. This edition features the excellent original translation and a sensitive abridgment. 304pp. 6⅛ x 9¼. 0-486-45789-3

LILITH: A Romance, George MacDonald. In this novel by the father of fantasy literature, a man travels through time to meet Adam and Eve and to explore humanity's fall from grace and ultimate redemption. 240pp. 5⅜ x 8½. 0-486-46818-6

THE LOST LANGUAGE OF SYMBOLISM, Harold Bayley. This remarkable book reveals the hidden meaning behind familiar images and words, from the origins of Santa Claus to the fleur-de-lys, drawing from mythology, folklore, religious texts, and fairy tales. 1,418 illustrations. 784pp. 5⅜ x 8½. 0-486-44787-1

MACBETH, William Shakespeare. A Scottish nobleman murders the king in order to succeed to the throne. Tortured by his conscience and fearful of discovery, he becomes tangled in a web of treachery and deceit that ultimately spells his doom. 96pp. 5³⁄₁₆ x 8¼. 0-486-27802-6

MAKING AUTHENTIC CRAFTSMAN FURNITURE: Instructions and Plans for 62 Projects, Gustav Stickley. Make authentic reproductions of handsome, functional, durable furniture: tables, chairs, wall cabinets, desks, a hall tree, and more. Construction plans with drawings, schematics, dimensions, and lumber specs reprinted from 1900s *The Craftsman* magazine. 128pp. 8⅛ x 11. 0-486-25000-8

MATHEMATICS FOR THE NONMATHEMATICIAN, Morris Kline. Erudite and entertaining overview follows development of mathematics from ancient Greeks to present. Topics include logic and mathematics, the fundamental concept, differential calculus, probability theory, much more. Exercises and problems. 641pp. 5⅜ x 8½. 0-486-24823-2

MEMOIRS OF AN ARABIAN PRINCESS FROM ZANZIBAR, Emily Ruete. This 19th-century autobiography offers a rare inside look at the society surrounding a sultan's palace. A real-life princess in exile recalls her vanished world of harems, slave trading, and court intrigues. 288pp. 5⅜ x 8½. 0-486-47121-7

Browse over 9,000 books at www.doverpublications.com

THE METAMORPHOSIS AND OTHER STORIES, Franz Kafka. Excellent new English translations of title story (considered by many critics Kafka's most perfect work), plus "The Judgment," "In the Penal Colony," "A Country Doctor," and "A Report to an Academy." Note. 96pp. 5³⁄₁₆ x 8¼.
0-486-29030-1

MICROSCOPIC ART FORMS FROM THE PLANT WORLD, R. Anheisser. From undulating curves to complex geometrics, a world of fascinating images abound in this classic, illustrated survey of microscopic plants. Features 400 detailed illustrations of nature's minute but magnificent handiwork. The accompanying CD-ROM includes all of the images in the book. 128pp. 9 x 9.
0-486-46013-4

A MIDSUMMER NIGHT'S DREAM, William Shakespeare. Among the most popular of Shakespeare's comedies, this enchanting play humorously celebrates the vagaries of love as it focuses upon the intertwined romances of several pairs of lovers. Explanatory footnotes. 80pp. 5³⁄₁₆ x 8¼.
0-486-27067-X

THE MONEY CHANGERS, Upton Sinclair. Originally published in 1908, this cautionary novel from the author of *The Jungle* explores corruption within the American system as a group of power brokers joins forces for personal gain, triggering a crash on Wall Street. 192pp. 5⅜ x 8½.
0-486-46917-4

THE MOST POPULAR HOMES OF THE TWENTIES, William A. Radford. With a New Introduction by Daniel D. Reiff. Based on a rare 1925 catalog, this architectural showcase features floor plans, construction details, and photos of 26 homes, plus articles on entrances, porches, garages, and more. 250 illustrations, 21 color plates. 176pp. 8⅜ x 11.
0-486-47028-8

MY 66 YEARS IN THE BIG LEAGUES, Connie Mack. With a New Introduction by Rich Westcott. A Founding Father of modern baseball, Mack holds the record for most wins — and losses — by a major league manager. Enhanced by 70 photographs, his warmhearted autobiography is populated by many legends of the game. 288pp. 5⅜ x 8½.
0-486-47184-5

NARRATIVE OF THE LIFE OF FREDERICK DOUGLASS, Frederick Douglass. Douglass's graphic depictions of slavery, harrowing escape to freedom, and life as a newspaper editor, eloquent orator, and impassioned abolitionist. 96pp. 5³⁄₁₆ x 8¼.
0-486-28499-9

THE NIGHTLESS CITY: Geisha and Courtesan Life in Old Tokyo, J. E. de Becker. This unsurpassed study from 100 years ago ventured into Tokyo's red-light district to survey geisha and courtesan life and offer meticulous descriptions of training, dress, social hierarchy, and erotic practices. 49 black-and-white illustrations; 2 maps. 496pp. 5⅜ x 8½.
0-486-45563-7

THE ODYSSEY, Homer. Excellent prose translation of ancient epic recounts adventures of the homeward-bound Odysseus. Fantastic cast of gods, giants, cannibals, sirens, other supernatural creatures — true classic of Western literature. 256pp. 5³⁄₁₆ x 8¼.
0-486-40654-7

OEDIPUS REX, Sophocles. Landmark of Western drama concerns the catastrophe that ensues when King Oedipus discovers he has inadvertently killed his father and married his mother. Masterly construction, dramatic irony. Explanatory footnotes. 64pp. 5³⁄₁₆ x 8¼.
0-486-26877-2

ONCE UPON A TIME: The Way America Was, Eric Sloane. Nostalgic text and drawings brim with gentle philosophies and descriptions of how we used to live — self-sufficiently — on the land, in homes, and among the things built by hand. 44 line illustrations. 64pp. 8⅜ x 11.
0-486-44411-2

CATALOG OF DOVER BOOKS

ONE OF OURS, Willa Cather. The Pulitzer Prize–winning novel about a young Nebraskan looking for something to believe in. Alienated from his parents, rejected by his wife, he finds his destiny on the bloody battlefields of World War I. 352pp. 5³⁄₁₆ x 8¼. 0-486-45599-8

ORIGAMI YOU CAN USE: 27 Practical Projects, Rick Beech. Origami models can be more than decorative, and this unique volume shows how! The 27 practical projects include a CD case, frame, napkin ring, and dish. Easy instructions feature 400 two-color illustrations. 96pp. 8¼ x 11. 0-486-47057-1

OTHELLO, William Shakespeare. Towering tragedy tells the story of a Moorish general who earns the enmity of his ensign Iago when he passes him over for a promotion. Masterly portrait of an archvillain. Explanatory footnotes. 112pp. 5³⁄₁₆ x 8¼. 0-486-29097-2

PARADISE LOST, John Milton. Notes by John A. Himes. First published in 1667, Paradise Lost ranks among the greatest of English literature's epic poems. It's a sublime retelling of Adam and Eve's fall from grace and expulsion from Eden. Notes by John A. Himes. 480pp. 5³⁄₁₆ x 8¼. 0-486-44287-X

PASSING, Nella Larsen. Married to a successful physician and prominently ensconced in society, Irene Redfield leads a charmed existence — until a chance encounter with a childhood friend who has been "passing for white." 112pp. 5⅜ x 8½. 0-486-43713-2

PERSPECTIVE DRAWING FOR BEGINNERS, Len A. Doust. Doust carefully explains the roles of lines, boxes, and circles, and shows how visualizing shapes and forms can be used in accurate depictions of perspective. One of the most concise introductions available. 33 illustrations. 64pp. 5⅜ x 8½. 0-486-45149-6

PERSPECTIVE MADE EASY, Ernest R. Norling. Perspective is easy; yet, surprisingly few artists know the simple rules that make it so. Remedy that situation with this simple, step-by-step book, the first devoted entirely to the topic. 256 illustrations. 224pp. 5⅜ x 8½. 0-486-40473-0

THE PICTURE OF DORIAN GRAY, Oscar Wilde. Celebrated novel involves a handsome young Londoner who sinks into a life of depravity. His body retains perfect youth and vigor while his recent portrait reflects the ravages of his crime and sensuality. 176pp. 5³⁄₁₆ x 8¼. 0-486-27807-7

PRIDE AND PREJUDICE, Jane Austen. One of the most universally loved and admired English novels, an effervescent tale of rural romance transformed by Jane Austen's art into a witty, shrewdly observed satire of English country life. 272pp. 5³⁄₁₆ x 8¼. 0-486-28473-5

THE PRINCE, Niccolò Machiavelli. Classic, Renaissance-era guide to acquiring and maintaining political power. Today, nearly 500 years after it was written, this calculating prescription for autocratic rule continues to be much read and studied. 80pp. 5³⁄₁₆ x 8¼. 0-486-27274-5

QUICK SKETCHING, Carl Cheek. A perfect introduction to the technique of "quick sketching." Drawing upon an artist's immediate emotional responses, this is an extremely effective means of capturing the essential form and features of a subject. More than 100 black-and-white illustrations throughout. 48pp. 11 x 8¼. 0-486-46608-6

RANCH LIFE AND THE HUNTING TRAIL, Theodore Roosevelt. Illustrated by Frederic Remington. Beautifully illustrated by Remington, Roosevelt's celebration of the Old West recounts his adventures in the Dakota Badlands of the 1880s, from roundups to Indian encounters to hunting bighorn sheep. 208pp. 6¼ x 9¼. 0-486-47340-6

Browse over 9,000 books at www.doverpublications.com

THE RED BADGE OF COURAGE, Stephen Crane. Amid the nightmarish chaos of a Civil War battle, a young soldier discovers courage, humility, and, perhaps, wisdom. Uncanny re-creation of actual combat. Enduring landmark of American fiction. 112pp. 5³⁄₁₆ x 8¼. 0-486-26465-3

RELATIVITY SIMPLY EXPLAINED, Martin Gardner. One of the subject's clearest, most entertaining introductions offers lucid explanations of special and general theories of relativity, gravity, and spacetime, models of the universe, and more. 100 illustrations. 224pp. 5⅜ x 8½. 0-486-29315-7

REMBRANDT DRAWINGS: 116 Masterpieces in Original Color, Rembrandt van Rijn. This deluxe hardcover edition features drawings from throughout the Dutch master's prolific career. Informative captions accompany these beautifully reproduced landscapes, biblical vignettes, figure studies, animal sketches, and portraits. 128pp. 8⅜ x 11. 0-486-46149-1

THE ROAD NOT TAKEN AND OTHER POEMS, Robert Frost. A treasury of Frost's most expressive verse. In addition to the title poem: "An Old Man's Winter Night," "In the Home Stretch," "Meeting and Passing," "Putting in the Seed," many more. All complete and unabridged. 64pp. 5³⁄₁₆ x 8¼. 0-486-27550-7

ROMEO AND JULIET, William Shakespeare. Tragic tale of star-crossed lovers, feuding families and timeless passion contains some of Shakespeare's most beautiful and lyrical love poetry. Complete, unabridged text with explanatory footnotes. 96pp. 5³⁄₁₆ x 8¼. 0-486-27557-4

SANDITON AND THE WATSONS: Austen's Unfinished Novels, Jane Austen. Two tantalizing incomplete stories revisit Austen's customary milieu of courtship and venture into new territory, amid guests at a seaside resort. Both are worth reading for pleasure and study. 112pp. 5⅜ x 8½. 0-486-45793-1

THE SCARLET LETTER, Nathaniel Hawthorne. With stark power and emotional depth, Hawthorne's masterpiece explores sin, guilt, and redemption in a story of adultery in the early days of the Massachusetts Colony. 192pp. 5³⁄₁₆ x 8¼. 0-486-28048-9

THE SEASONS OF AMERICA PAST, Eric Sloane. Seventy-five illustrations depict cider mills and presses, sleds, pumps, stump-pulling equipment, plows, and other elements of America's rural heritage. A section of old recipes and household hints adds additional color. 160pp. 8⅜ x 11. 0-486-44220-9

SELECTED CANTERBURY TALES, Geoffrey Chaucer. Delightful collection includes the General Prologue plus three of the most popular tales: "The Knight's Tale," "The Miller's Prologue and Tale," and "The Wife of Bath's Prologue and Tale." In modern English. 144pp. 5³⁄₁₆ x 8¼. 0-486-28241-4

SELECTED POEMS, Emily Dickinson. Over 100 best-known, best-loved poems by one of America's foremost poets, reprinted from authoritative early editions. No comparable edition at this price. Index of first lines. 64pp. 5³⁄₁₆ x 8¼. 0-486-26466-1

SIDDHARTHA, Hermann Hesse. Classic novel that has inspired generations of seekers. Blending Eastern mysticism and psychoanalysis, Hesse presents a strikingly original view of man and culture and the arduous process of self-discovery, reconciliation, harmony, and peace. 112pp. 5³⁄₁₆ x 8¼. 0-486-40653-9

SKETCHING OUTDOORS, Leonard Richmond. This guide offers beginners step-by-step demonstrations of how to depict clouds, trees, buildings, and other outdoor sights. Explanations of a variety of techniques include shading and constructional drawing. 48pp. 11 x 8¼. 0-486-46922-0

Browse over 9,000 books at www.doverpublications.com

SMALL HOUSES OF THE FORTIES: With Illustrations and Floor Plans, Harold E. Group. 56 floor plans and elevations of houses that originally cost less than $15,000 to build. Recommended by financial institutions of the era, they range from Colonials to Cape Cods. 144pp. 8⅜ x 11.   0-486-45598-X

SOME CHINESE GHOSTS, Lafcadio Hearn. Rooted in ancient Chinese legends, these richly atmospheric supernatural tales are recounted by an expert in Oriental lore. Their originality, power, and literary charm will captivate readers of all ages. 96pp. 5⅜ x 8½.   0-486-46306-0

SONGS FOR THE OPEN ROAD: Poems of Travel and Adventure, Edited by The American Poetry & Literacy Project. More than 80 poems by 50 American and British masters celebrate real and metaphorical journeys. Poems by Whitman, Byron, Millay, Sandburg, Langston Hughes, Emily Dickinson, Robert Frost, Shelley, Tennyson, Yeats, many others. Note. 80pp. 5³⁄₁₆ x 8¼.   0-486-40646-6

SPOON RIVER ANTHOLOGY, Edgar Lee Masters. An American poetry classic, in which former citizens of a mythical midwestern town speak touchingly from the grave of the thwarted hopes and dreams of their lives. 144pp. 5³⁄₁₆ x 8¼.
0-486-27275-3

STAR LORE: Myths, Legends, and Facts, William Tyler Olcott. Captivating retellings of the origins and histories of ancient star groups include Pegasus, Ursa Major, Pleiades, signs of the zodiac, and other constellations. "Classic." — *Sky & Telescope*. 58 illustrations. 544pp. 5⅜ x 8½.   0-486-43581-4

THE STRANGE CASE OF DR. JEKYLL AND MR. HYDE, Robert Louis Stevenson. This intriguing novel, both fantasy thriller and moral allegory, depicts the struggle of two opposing personalities — one essentially good, the other evil — for the soul of one man. 64pp. 5³⁄₁₆ x 8¼.   0-486-26688-5

SURVIVAL HANDBOOK: The Official U.S. Army Guide, Department of the Army. This special edition of the Army field manual is geared toward civilians. An essential companion for campers and all lovers of the outdoors, it constitutes the most authoritative wilderness guide. 288pp. 5³⁄₁₆ x 8¼.   0-486-46184-X

A TALE OF TWO CITIES, Charles Dickens. Against the backdrop of the French Revolution, Dickens unfolds his masterpiece of drama, adventure, and romance about a man falsely accused of treason. Excitement and derring-do in the shadow of the guillotine. 304pp. 5³⁄₁₆ x 8¼.   0-486-40651-2

TEN PLAYS, Anton Chekhov. *The Sea Gull, Uncle Vanya, The Three Sisters, The Cherry Orchard,* and *Ivanov,* plus 5 one-act comedies: *The Anniversary, An Unwilling Martyr, The Wedding, The Bear,* and *The Proposal.* 336pp. 5³⁄₁₆ x 8¼.   0-486-46560-8

THE FLYING INN, G. K. Chesterton. Hilarious romp in which pub owner Humphrey Hump and friend take to the road in a donkey cart filled with rum and cheese, inveighing against Prohibition and other "oppressive forms of modernity." 320pp. 5⅜ x 8½.   0-486-41910-X

THIRTY YEARS THAT SHOOK PHYSICS: The Story of Quantum Theory, George Gamow. Lucid, accessible introduction to the influential theory of energy and matter features careful explanations of Dirac's anti-particles, Bohr's model of the atom, and much more. Numerous drawings. 1966 edition. 240pp. 5⅜ x 8½. 0-486-24895-X

TREASURE ISLAND, Robert Louis Stevenson. Classic adventure story of a perilous sea journey, a mutiny led by the infamous Long John Silver, and a lethal scramble for buried treasure — seen through the eyes of cabin boy Jim Hawkins. 160pp. 5³⁄₁₆ x 8¼.
0-486-27559-0

CATALOG OF DOVER BOOKS

LIGHT AND SHADE: A Classic Approach to Three-Dimensional Drawing, Mrs. Mary P. Merrifield. Handy reference clearly demonstrates principles of light and shade by revealing effects of common daylight, sunshine, and candle or artificial light on geometrical solids. 13 plates. 64pp. 5⅜ x 8½. 0-486-44143-1

ASTROLOGY AND ASTRONOMY: A Pictorial Archive of Signs and Symbols, Ernst and Johanna Lehner. Treasure trove of stories, lore, and myth, accompanied by more than 300 rare illustrations of planets, the Milky Way, signs of the zodiac, comets, meteors, and other astronomical phenomena. 192pp. 8⅜ x 11. 0-486-43981-X

JEWELRY MAKING: Techniques for Metal, Tim McCreight. Easy-to-follow instructions and carefully executed illustrations describe tools and techniques, use of gems and enamels, wire inlay, casting, and other topics. 72 line illustrations and diagrams. 176pp. 8¼ x 10⅞. 0-486-44043-5

MAKING BIRDHOUSES: Easy and Advanced Projects, Gladstone Califf. Easy-to-follow instructions include diagrams for everything from a one-room house for bluebirds to a forty-two-room structure for purple martins. 56 plates; 4 figures. 80pp. 8¾ x 6⅜. 0-486-44183-0

LITTLE BOOK OF LOG CABINS: How to Build and Furnish Them, William S. Wicks. Handy how-to manual, with instructions and illustrations for building cabins in the Adirondack style, fireplaces, stairways, furniture, beamed ceilings, and more. 102 line drawings. 96pp. 8¾ x 6⅜. 0-486-44259-4

THE SEASONS OF AMERICA PAST, Eric Sloane. From "sugaring time" and strawberry picking to Indian summer and fall harvest, a whole year's activities described in charming prose and enhanced with 79 of the author's own illustrations. 160pp. 8¼ x 11. 0-486-44220-9

THE METROPOLIS OF TOMORROW, Hugh Ferriss. Generous, prophetic vision of the metropolis of the future, as perceived in 1929. Powerful illustrations of towering structures, wide avenues, and rooftop parks–all features in many of today's modern cities. 59 illustrations. 144pp. 8¼ x 11. 0-486-43727-2

THE PATH TO ROME, Hilaire Belloc. This 1902 memoir abounds in lively vignettes from a vanished time, recounting a pilgrimage on foot across the Alps and Apennines in order to "see all Europe which the Christian Faith has saved." 77 of the author's original line drawings complement his sparkling prose. 272pp. 5⅜ x 8½. 0-486-44001-X

THE HISTORY OF RASSELAS: Prince of Abissinia, Samuel Johnson. Distinguished English writer attacks eighteenth-century optimism and man's unrealistic estimates of what life has to offer. 112pp. 5⅜ x 8½. 0-486-44094-X

A VOYAGE TO ARCTURUS, David Lindsay. A brilliant flight of pure fancy, where wild creatures crowd the fantastic landscape and demented torturers dominate victims with their bizarre mental powers. 272pp. 5⅜ x 8½. 0-486-44198-9

Paperbound unless otherwise indicated. Available at your book dealer, online at **www.doverpublications.com**, or by writing to Dept. GI, Dover Publications, Inc., 31 East 2nd Street, Mineola, NY 11501. For current price information or for free catalogs (please indicate field of interest), write to Dover Publications or log on to **www.doverpublications.com** and see every Dover book in print. Dover publishes more than 500 books each year on science, elementary and advanced mathematics, biology, music, art, literary history, social sciences, and other areas.